Walks of Seven West Cork Islands

By Damien Enright

A Merlin Press Publication

Published by Merlin Press

© Damien Enright

ISBN 1-902631-08-0

Designed by Sean O'Leary
Illustrations by Christine Thery
Cover photo by Pierce Hickey Limited
Photos by Elishea Nicholson
Layout and maps by Matthew Enright

MERLIN PRESS
Courtmacsherry, Co. Cork
Tel/Fax: +353 023 46045

Contents

Walks through some of Ireland's most beautiful and romantic scenery on the Atlantic islands off Ireland's south-west coast.

Dedicated to:
My patient wife, children, friends and dog
who have made life's roads a pleasure
and lightened my steps on the way

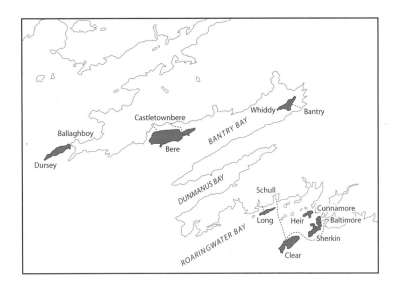

Introduction

The thrill of a day on the islands begins at the ferry, or the cable car if one is going to Dursey. As the mainland recedes, there is the sense that the everyday world is another country we have left behind. The islands ahead move in another time; for those not old enough to remember, we can say this is what Ireland was like before the traffic and the hurry, a less busy, more gracious place.

Those islanders who did not emigrate to England or America had to find comfort in earth, sea, weather and religion; there was food for the spirit, if not always for the stomach. David S Quin's magnificent poem Lucht an Oileain (People of the Islands) captures the spirit of the islanders better than I could hope to. He says:

for they dwelt upon a rock in the sea and not in a shining metropolis
and lived off the pick of the strand, the hunt of the hill, the fish
in the sea the wool off sheep, and packets full of dollars...
they were full of sunlight and mist, wind and stone, rain and rock,
but the Atlantic ocean would not pay them a regular salary...

The spirit of those people, who colonised and turned to good use patches of sea-locked rock and land all along the West Cork coast - all around the coasts of Ireland - has left its testament in the lonely crofts and cottages, the abandoned potato drills and lazy beds, and the ruins on small islands long abandoned. It is heartening to know that, in this new millennium, their world is enjoying a revival. The natives who remained are a determined people; through centuries of often grinding hardship, they 'hung on' and now look forward a vibrant future in island industry, crafts and tourism. Meanwhile, newcomers arrive to live amongst them, new faces and new lifestyles. They bring hopes and dreams, some capital and a respect for the way of life. They come to share the peace, understanding the value of the unique island environment and the nurture to be found in self-reliance.

For visitors, the West Cork islands provide superb walking and a wealth of avian and marine fauna. Beside the paths and bohreens, wild flowers bloom in a profusion rarely seen in mainland Ireland. The only sound is bird song, and the hum of bees. Humans are few; traffic is non-existent. The air is laced with ozone, and immensities of mountain, sea and sky surround us.

SOURCES

It was Séamus Ó Drisceoil, of Oileán Chléire, who initiated this book. He came to me in 2004 with the idea, and his enthusiasm was infectious. We weren't sure how many copies it would sell, but we hoped that in a small way it would help in the ongoing revitalisation of the West Cork islands, and in bringing these lovely, unspoiled places to the attention of the mainland Irish and our visitors from overseas.

I am in debt to many others who helped and advised me. They, the writers, historians, folklorists and people of the islands are really the authors. It is their book. I am privileged to have been asked to compile it.

BOOKS

Discover Dursey by Penny Durell, Ballinacarriga Books, Allihies. Co. Cork.

Heir Island, its history and people by Eugene Daly, Leap, Co. Cork

A Short History of Bere Island by Ted O'Sullivan, Inisgragy Books, Cork

Cape Clear Island Heritage Trail Dr Éamon Lankford et al, published by Comharchumann Chléire Teo and Cape Clear Museum

The Mizen Journal, articles by Mary Mackay on Long Island publ. Mizen Archaeological and Historical Society

The Ecology of the Rocky Shores of Sherkin Island by Gillian Bishop and *The Wild Plants of Sherkin, Cape Clear and adjacent islands of West Cork* ed. John Akeroyd, both publ. Sherkin Island Marine Station

The Natural History of Cape Clear by JTR Sharrock. Available at the Tourist Information Centre.

MY THANKS TO:

Tim O'Leary, Larry Burke. Alex O'Donovan, Sean Desmond (Whiddy) Mary O'Driscoll, Steve Wing, Séamus Ó Drisceoil (Cape Clear), Ann Finch (Dursey), Colm Harrington, John Walsh (Bere Island), John Shelley, (Long Island). Also to Allanah Hopkin, Ann Barry, Marie Enright, for good company and editorial help. There are many more with whom I had a casual chat on the roadside or on a ferry boat. My gratitude to them, too.

A note on walking.

The Irish are big on walking. If there is one thing we have plenty of, it is back roads and fresh air.

There are the power walkers, the Walking Women of Ireland, plugging along country roads with hips and shoulders swinging, out for the exercise after an already much-exercised day. The glow of their cheeks and the litheness of their stride attests the beneficial effects of 'exercise walking'.

Irish men, on the other hand, seem oblivious to walking's cosmetic effect, an unfortunate oversight on their part. Males are not seen striding along country lanes. When we do see a male abroad, he is generally being pulled along at a heart-stopping pace by two fist-fulls of dog leads, his greyhounds taking him for a run, rather than the other way around. Other encounters will involve men in caps, with fags in mouth and pockets full of fivers, out following the road bowling, after which they will walk miles.

There are the hill walkers and long-distance route marchers, doughty folk in serious boots, with ashplants, maps and small rucksacks. To them, we owe the opening up of green roads and byways, and the mapping of mountain trails not trodden since the ancient Celts made their way across country via uplands, the plains being covered with a dense growth of trees.

I, myself, do not power walk, greyhound follow, or road bowl wager. I walk for the curiosity and the uplift, the wonderments of the wayside and the 'high' of the free-flowing endorphins released after twenty minutes on the hoof. I am not so much a slow walker as one who is waylaid by the roadside attractions. Curiosity, atmosphere or amazement delays me, and while the company forges ahead, I am left behind, in thrall.

The walks outlined in this book are for walkers such as I. They take, generally, just a couple of hours but can easily be stretched to fill half a day. They are perfect for a weekend afternoon or a holiday meander.

They will, hopefully, stimulate my perambulating neighbours towards new horizons and inform visitors of the lovely land that awaits just off the tourist trail. I cannot imagine these local by-ways ever becoming crowded. We may in time meet a party of ardent Japanese, led by a person with a flag, or stout Austrians in lederhosen and braces singing "Falderee-Falderah". They will be sure of a welcome. We Irish delight in showing off our land.

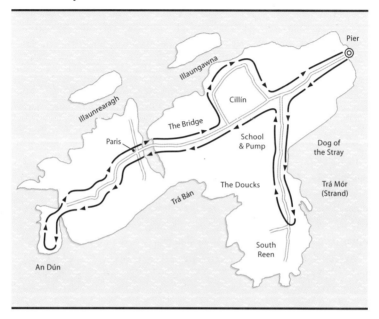

Heir Island Walk

Location, access and island life: Heir Island (OS Sheet 88; we start at GR 012285) lies north west of Baltimore in Roaringwater Bay. The shortest crossing is from Cunnamore Pier (see Ferry Schedules) but ferries also cross from both Baltimore and Schull. Heir is 2.5km long by 1.5km wide, (roughly a mile and a half by a mile) with a population of about 25, a third of them native islanders, the rest 'blow-ins' who have made their home there and brought new life; they are artists, chefs, boat builders, sailing school proprietors and so on. Today, there is a restaurant, B&B accommodation, a public phone box, a sailing school and a shop on the island. Visitors cross in summer to enjoy the beaches.

A marvellous book, *Heir Island, its history and people*, written by Eugene Daly and published in 2005, provided me with a volume of information only a small part of which can be included in this short essay. To anyone interested in Heir and the Roaringwater Bay islands, I would highly recommend this watershed work. It is a definitive record of the islands and their unique communities.

The walk, description and distance: The walk takes us to the length of the island, with spurs to north and south. Thedistance is 8 km. (5 mls.); the going is easy, with no steep hills. Heir is a gentle island, sheltered and less exposed than others in this book. There are delightful views in every direction and the sense of getting-away-from-it-all is powerful. There is much history, and good bathing beaches.

Walking conditions: Easy going. Island roads all the way.

An introduction.

Many people misunderstand the name Heir Island and think it will be a redoubt of *Lepus timidus hibernicus*, the long-legged Irish hare. In fact, it was so named for a long-ago heir to the leadership of the O'Driscolls. It is still called Inis Uí Drisceoil, O'Driscoll's Island, although nobody of that name live there now. Before the arrival of the McCarthys (of which there are plenty, in Heir) and O'Mahoneys, the O'Driscoll's were the most powerful clan on the southern seaboard. It is likely they, like other Irish tribes, were settled in the region before the Celts came. For centuries, they dominated the sea from Kinsale to Kenmare and no boat could fish, land cargo or trade along that coast without paying the O'Driscolls a levy. This brought them considerable wealth; in 1569, no less than two hundred Spanish boats were in their waters, each paying its fee to O'Driscoll Mor, whose thirty-oared galleon and other craft patrolled the seas. O'Driscoll castles and strongholds commanded the islands and the shores of Roaringwater Bay.

Itinerary.

(1) We arrive at the pier; usually, there is not a soul to be seen. Before starting up the road, we can go left on a small path that leads to a landing place of eight broad stone steps hand-carved into the rock in the 19th century or before, a testimony to the aspirations and industry of the islanders.

As we start out along the main island road, going south-west, the complete absence of traffic and the silence defines this as a place apart from the mainland. On a sunny October day, the roadside blackberries are warm and fat and the juice tastes like wine. In April, the almond scent of the French gorse hangs heavy in the air when the blossom is baking in the sun. The hillocks in the roadside fields are colonised by dwarf Irish gorse, gold in late summer but, unlike its continental cousin, flowerless otherwise.

The phone box has a bolt on the door, possibly to keep it closed in wild weather. We pass through cuttings where the shale is exposed and, in summer, capped with an orange and purple carpet of gorse and heather. The yellow flag iris, tall and elegant, with distinctive flat, sword shaped leaves, grows in the marshy ground, flowering from May to July; it was a heraldic device in the former royal arms of France. Pink cuckoo flowers bloom on wet patches on the roadside. .A cuckoo heard on Heir seems louder and sweeter than on the mainland, perhaps because of the clearness of the air.

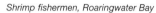

Shrimp fishermen, Roaringwater Bay

We see Clear Island, and its two hills, off to the left. To the right, seen over an ivy-grown shed and a bright hedge of fuchsia, is the islet of Skeam East, abandoned in 1958, with a herd of goats grazing and a substantial house with a chimney at either end. But for a few trees, the island is very bare. On the mainland, Mount Gabriel rises to the north west, the twin domes on the summit catching the sun.

There are robust artichokes in a wayside garden, a testimony to the mildness of the climate. Trees grow along the the roadside, and there are colonies of polypody and rustyback ferns on the ditches. Polypodys have no feathery fronds, but a series of broad 'teeth', and the reproductive spores are on the back of the leaf, neatly arranged, small, orange dots. Great blazes of orange montbretia flowers light up the verges in July and August.

We pass the acclaimed Heir Island Restaurant; in summer, they will arrange for a boat to carry you over for dinner, and take you home. Pheasants forage in the plantation alongside the road, and suddenly take flight from under one's feet, making one's heart stop. Ten kilometres north east, we see Kilcoe Castle, which, under the command of an O'Driscoll, was the last castle in West Cork to surrender to the English after the Irish defeat at Kinsale, 1601.

(2) We take a left turning, heading south. At first, pines edge the road. Pines are widely grown on the islands as shelter belts, generally Austrian pines, with straight, spine-tipped needles, grouped in pairs, or Monterey pines, from the Pacific North America, with needles in pairs and asymmetrical cones. There is fuchsia in the hedges, and wildflowers on the verges, from celandine and violets in early spring to ox-eye daisies in late autumn. The road winds down to the sea and there are views over Sherkin to the Signal Tower (called "Spain Tower") above Baltimore. Such towers, each within view of two others, were erected in 1804 to ring the south coast with an early-warning system for fear the French would invade, as they had in 1796 and 1798. A signal fire lit on one would alert those nearest, and thus along the chain.

We reach a white sand beach, Trá Mór. The northern side is known as the Dog of the Stray because a phantom dog was often seen here, sometimes the size of a cow. A stream issues from a reed bed and lake behind it, and we cross a bridge to Trá an Uisce, the Strand of the Water, and Trá Báirneach, the strand of the limpets. Their conical shells can be found in the sand, with the shells of dog cockle, clam, wild oysters and the scabbard-like shells of razorfish. Mallard cruise the lake, and herons hunt in the shallows. Sea mayweed, with its daisy-like flowers, grows on the shingle and, in May, tussocks of sea pink are in full flower. There is a third strand, and beyond it, a grassy track goes up to the right. Previously, one could continue over rough land and arrive at the western end of the dorsal road to make a loop walk back to the pier. A gate with a No Entry sign now bars the way but one hopes that when the owner, who lives in America, learns of the Supreme Court decision (2005) enshrining protection for landowners against personal injury claims, he may allow walkers to pass.

The shop, Heir Island

(3) Leaving Trá Mór, we return the way we have come. Back on the dorsal road, we turn left and, after passing a road going down to the right we soon reach the Heir Island National School, built in 1900. In the mid 1800s, there were two schools on Heir, the old National School and one run by the Island Society under Rev. Edward Spring, who dispensed soup to those who enrolled in his school and joined his Protestant congregation. The recipients were called 'soupers', a pejorative term. At the height of the Famine, 1847-1850, it would seem there were sometimes more pupils at Spring's school but numbers fell once the Famine was over, and the school closed. Then, there were upward to 100 school children on the island. By 1945, there were less than 30, and the school was closed in 1976.

The gate is locked, the gate piers blotched with yellow lichens. The yard is overgrown with fuchsia and wildflowers. One can imagine the activity that once was here and the excited voices of the children. Beside the school is a rusting pump. Over the years, how many small heads must have inclined beneath it to catch a mouthful of its water on long-ago summer days.

A 'green lane' goes down to the right. For now, we ignore it and continue straight ahead.

Sheep are often left to graze on outer islands

During the Famine, the population of Heir fell from 358 to 288. Before the potato failure, even the smallest, most inhospitable islands held small communities. These often fared better than those on the mainland where, tragically, in order to survive, many pawned their boats in the first blight-stricken years and then could no longer fish. On Heir, the women and children lived on shellfish and seaweed, leaving the Indian corn for the men who, to earn Famine Relief for the family, had to work, however weak.

The road rises slightly. In a field on the right, a wooden cross and small upright stones marks a cilín where unbaptised children, unidentified bodies washed in by the sea and the bodies of suicides were buried. The lonely hills running west from Mount Gabriel are very clear from here.

We go downhill towards a pretty inlet, spanned by a humpback bridge, with a hamlet of small houses beyond , and a few boats drawn up on the shore. This is Paris, derived from 'pallace', referring to a 'fish pallace' built here, one of three on the island. Many were built along the West Cork coast when pilchards arrived in their millions each summer and were harvested by locals and boats from Britain, France and Spain. In the pallaces, 'train oil', for lamps and for tanning leather, was extracted using large presses. The inlet almost cuts the island into two parts. Oystercatchers, with their black and white plumage, red bills and legs, and curlews, with long down-curved bills, pick over the mud at low tide, and there are bright cushions of sea pinks in May.

The National School, built 1900, Heir Island

We cross the bridge and continue uphill. Tracks pass between the houses and go down to the sea beyond. We soon get views Skeam West, abandoned in 1940, and Barnacleeve Gap, on the mainland east of Mount Gabriel. In the early Christian period, Skeam West (Inis Céim) had a wooden church built by St. Céim, brother of St. Ciarán (see Clear Island Walk). In medieval times, this was replaced by a stone church; the ruins are still there. Inis Céim was a holy island, and dead from all around the bay were buried here, the earliest graves dated to C430 AD. The land was good. Although lashed by waves in bad weather, the anchorage was much safer than in Skeam East.

The road passes between houses and winds around a fine dwelling painted in brilliant azure, with big fuchsia hedges resplendent in autumn. It continues between marshy fields and we can see the Marine Station on Sherkin and Gascanane Sound, between Sherkin and Clear, where islanders would long-line for gurnard, the fish that grunts. 'Gurnard' comes from the French, to 'growl' or 'grunt'. They can make such a racket as they pass below the surface that they can be heard by a fishing boat above.

(4) Shortly, the road becomes a grassy track. Grey sea-ivory lichen colonises the low stone walls, and a rusting iron harrow, overgrown and picturesque, lies against one, over which we have a near view of Cape Clear. On the other side, we see the beacon at the east end of Long Island, and a signal tower at Brow Head, far west.

We pass through a style onto the headland, An Dún. A *dún* is a fort and there was probably a promontory fort of the pre-Celtic O'Driscolls. Steep cliffs enclose a pebble beach, with crystal clear water; one needs to watch one's step. The ground is blanketed with bell heather, dwarf gorse and bracken but the scalp is bare. The view, over the Calf Islands, to the Western Ocean, is breathtaking. When the sun, like a heavenly searchlight, breaks through the clouds and pinpoints the Fastnet out on the horizon, one can all but hear celestial choirs. In summer, mackerel shoals ripple the surface like fairy winds, and gannets, big white birds with black wing tips, power-dive into the sea in the midst of them. There is no finer place to be than on the Dún of a summer evening, as the sun sinks into the sea.

(5) We return the way we came. We have been east, south, and west; we now go north as far as the land allows. At the top of a hill, just before a house with substantial corrugated iron barns, we take the 'green lane' with high ditches that goes left down to the sea. We reach a pebbly strand and, in front of it, the Shrule (or channel) and Illaungowna, sometime grazed by goats.

(6) We swing right, in the direction of some houses and trees, and meet a tarred lane. At the time of writing, there are plans to have a sailing school here, and a shop/cafe in summer. The tarred lane takes us back to the dorsal road, and we turn left for the pier.

© Start point

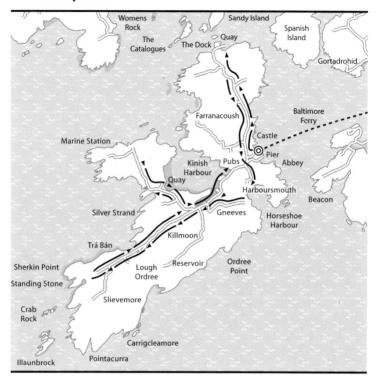

Sherkin Island Walk

Location, access and island life: The old name for Sherkin is Inis Archáin, Archain's Island. This may come from orca, the killer whale, as in the case of Orkney, off the Scottish coast, or it may mean the island of sea-pigs or porpoises; arcáin was the Irish word for these. Others believe it derives from the name Ciarán as in St. Ciarán of nearby Cape Clear Island. The source is uncertain, indeed 'arcane'.

The island (OS Sheet 88, centre at GR 0225) is some 5km (3 mls) long and 2km (1.2mls) wide, with a resident population of about 100. The land is good, but for the south shore and the slopes of Slievemore, and there are pleasant bathing beaches. The ferry takes fifteen minutes from Baltimore. A seal often surfaces in the Baltimore dock, watching the people come and go. The ferry has a notice saying dogs are welcome, provided owners are kept on a leash.

The walk, description and distance: We set out from the pier on the east of the island, where the ferry comes in, and walk to the northern, southern and western extremes. The total distance is 9 miles, easily divided into shorter sections. A morning or early afternoon crossing, returning to the mainland on the last boat, allows time for longer or shorter sections, even for the entire walk

Walking conditions: Most of the route follows the tarred roads, but there is little or no traffic; one may not meet a single car . There are off-road sections, so good boots are advisable.

An introduction.

Sherkin, with all but traffic-less roads has a pace of life which takes one back to the Ireland of the 1950s. Indoors, life is as modern as on the mainland but the island's byways seem suffused with a slower time. The absence of cars doesn't alone explain this; there is something 'apart' about Sherkin, perhaps that feeling of isolation from the material world which, until a few decades ago, prevailed throughout the island of Ireland.

As we approach the island, we see that the channel separating it from the mainland is steep-sided and deep, with a white beacon like a rocket ship on the mainland and a lighthouse on the cliffs on the Sherkin side. Black rocks, like small mountains, break the surface; the Clear Island ferry passes through this sound.

Arriving off an early afternoon boat, we have adequate time to walk the length and breadth of Sherkin, and to pause at suitable intervals to drink it in. If we arrive in the morning, we will also have time, weather permitting, for a swim, and a sundowner at one of the pubs before we catch the ferry. Let there be no hurry; just to sit on the small beach or stand on the slip and watch the small pollock threading through the weeds and the crabs waiting in ambush on the weedy wall is enough to while away time most pleasantly. When the children are young, and the tide is in, it is likely they will immensely enjoy diving into the deep, clear waters and will never want to go home.

Itinerary.

(1) A steep road leads up from the pier, past a ruined friary. Overnight visitors set off carrying their luggage; recently, a taxi service has been established, but nowhere is very far and many visitors opt to walk. Bird song and bee-hum pervade the air in summer, and swallows twitter on the wires. Butterflies seem tamer and more numerous.

At the time of writing, conservation work on the friary is ongoing. The work began in 1986, and the bell tower has since been repaired, with new oak floors and oak roof timbers. A Franciscan house founded by the O'Driscolls in about 1460, it was burnt in 1537 by Waterford raiders,

Ruined house, Sherkin

smarting from the expropriation of eighteen thousand gallons of wine by Fineen O'Driscoll from a Waterford-bound ship that sheltered in Baltimore harbour earlier that year. In retaliation, the merchants of Waterford sent a force of 400 men, led by an English adventurer . They 'invaded' Sherkin, seized the castle, and spent five days ravaging the island, burning the villages, abbey and castle, and scuttling or seizing the O'Driscoll fleet. The castle was rebuilt, but seized by Spaniards in 1602, after the final Irish defeat at Kinsale the previous year. Sir Fineen accommodated them, supplying artillery and ammunition. When the English seized it, Sir Fineen, who had played both sides, was lucky to lose only his lands and not his life. Once lord of many castles and the islands of Roaringwater Bay, he died destitute in his last remaining tower house at Lough Hyne. (More history of the O'Driscolls and Sir Fineen in the Heir Island Walk in this book and in Walks of Skibbereen in this series).

The plants on the earth-and-stone wall on our left as we walk towards the telephone box and the shop are worth notice. Here, amongst others, may be found Sherkin's only crop of Bird's Foot, a rare, small white flower of early March. There is also heath speedwell, germander speedwell, stonecrop, and various ferns. Sherkin has the largest flora of all the islands of the bay, the most trees and the best developed scrubland.

On the leylandii above the road on the right, opposite the abbey, one sees the effect of the prevailing winds. As we reach the junction, we take the road going right signposted for the Islander's Rest hotel and the Jolly Roger pub. The island silence is marvellous, if anything accentuated by the bird song. Birds are in profusion, all the familiar species, and grey crows (hooded crows) which may not be familiar to visitors from the UK.

(2) Just beyond The Islander's Rest, a right turn takes us down to the remains of Dunalong, The Fort of the Ships, an O'Driscoll castle, now a stumpy, ivy-covered tower. Wild parsley, growing on the walls, and black mustard, with its yellow flowers are, perhaps, survivors of an ancient kitchen garden. One might well imagine Sir Fineen, lord of the islands, proudly looking across at his tower house of Dunashad, The Fort of the Jewels, in Baltimore town, meanwhile perhaps enjoying a glass of misappropriated Waterford wine. Like Dunalong, Dunashad would be burnt in the retaliatory raid by the Waterford men, in 1537. Fineen rebuilt it, and it has recently been restored to its former glory. Before the Battle of Kinsale and the end of the old order, Sir Fineen, pirate and rover, was still rich from the fees the O'Driscoll's levied on any boat fishing between the Stags and Fastnet.

Back on the tarmac, the road winds gently north between high ditches colonised by harts tongue ferns, with waxy green leaves like straps or tongues, French gorse, primroses, foxgloves, yarrow and a host of other wild plants, each flowering in its season. There are wide views across the water to Ringarogy and Spanish Island, red with dead bracken in winter, where scattered sheep graze. In spring and summer, the background sounds are bird song and the humming of bees; it is worth watching for unusual birds, as rare migrants sometimes make a landfall here.

The sea below us is often calm, with the rocks jet black against the brilliant ultramarine. Shabby-looking cormorants stand silhouetted on the shore, hanging out their wings to dry. New houses are going up here and there, but Sherkin remains part of 'the peaceful kingdom' of nature. It isn't houses so much as cars that would destroy it.

Detail of Dunalong, The Fort of the Ships

Topping a small rise, we see rocks and islands laid out before us, Heir Island and its pier, the pier at Cunnamore, Sandy Island and The Catalogues. From late March, these are ablaze with gorse; beyond them are channels of bright water, blue hills and the bulk of Mount Gabriel where, nearly 4000 years ago, the pre-Celtic Irish mined copper before any other Europeans and, mixing it with tin from Cornwall, made bronze. Now, huge, white 'golf balls', monitoring North Atlantic air and sea traffic, top the summit.

The road leads down to a boat slip, called The Dock. A wide beach is exposed at low tide, and one can walk to the offshore islets. Small mullet cruise in the shallows and the cove is a delight for the amateur marine biologist or the child with a shrimping net. A Beginner's Guide to Ireland's Seashore, published by Sherkin Island Marine Station, is invaluable. For the expert, Gilian Bishop's Ecology of the Rocky Shores of Sherkin Island, also published by the Marine Station, provides a wealth of data.

Low water provides a chance to see most of the common seaweeds, each having its own niche and specific zone, nearer or further from the tide mark. Ten feet up the rock walls on the left, channelled wrack survives in the high water splash zone; moisture held in the channels on the fronds keeps it alive, unsubmerged, for days. At the base of the rocks, sugar kelp, like flattened barley sugar, and oarweed, a kelp with a strong stipe or stem, is submerged at all but the lowest tides. Nearby, almost the entire inshore flora may be found, including sea lettuce, laver and edible caragreen.

In summer, there are small fish, shannies and gobies, in the rock pools, and crabs and prawns. Clinging to the sides are liver-red beadlet anemones with brilliant blue 'beads' around the 'neck' from which the tentacles emerge; they tickle your fingers 'electrically' if you touch them. Millions of tiny, white acorn barnacles cling to the rocks, along with limpets, shaped like cones, periwinkles, with black, snail-like shells, and white dog whelks, with a groove at the shell mouth allowing a small 'snorkel' to be raised as they crawl over mud. They have a drill-like tongue and bore through the shells of mussels to suck out the soft body inside. We find shells on the beach with neat holes drilled in them.

Sherkin road

On the beach, sand masons, exotic marine worms, put up tubes of sand, fringed with a sandy mop to protect the delicate tentacles which they raise to filter food when the tide covers them. The spaghetti-like whorls of lugworms are everywhere, with a hole close by; the worm is a foot beneath the sand, roughly between the two.

Rocks above the tide line are colonised with white flowering scurvy grass, sea pinks, and lichens, especially grey-green Neptune's Beard (sea ivory) and orange xanthoria.

(3) We return to the friary corner the way we came. En route, we may notice items of interest that were hidden on the outward leg.

(4) At the corner, we turn right, passing a framed map of the island, and go left at the phone box, taking the sign for Horseshoe Harbour. We are now on a track, with a gate to the left, to the lighthouse and a private residence. We pass house ruins and Horseshoe Cottage, a B&B decorated with nets and net-balls. We go through a gate and shortly have a view down to the (usually) mirror-calm waters of Horseshoe Harbour. It is clear why it is described as a 'horseshoe'; it is a perfect amphitheatre, with its mouth opening to the sea.

We cross a stile and the path narrows to a grassy track. Foxgloves hang over it in June, and bees buzz busily in the sun trap of the lane. The heather- and gorse-covered slopes, and the deep blue of the harbour make this circuit idyllic in summer. A few pretty houses, accessible only on foot, look down on it. Blackthorn blooms over the water in March, whitethorn in May, montbretia in August, fuchsia into October - never a colourless day once spring arrives.

We go downhill. At the lowest point, there is a platform of soft grass over the sea, perfect for laying out a picnic of a summer day. In winter storms, it is an exciting spot from which to watch the waves breaking over the harbour mouth. A stream crosses the path, muddy in wet weather. As it climbs the slope to Gneeves, on the south side, the path becomes a stream bed in wet weather. As we gradually ascend, the small, neat, Sherkin lighthouse and keeper's cottage comes into view across the harbour. Reaching the crest, we come upon a shale road into a house. We turn right and set off downhill to join the main island road. We can see it below us. After a shower, it shines like a silver ribbon running straight south west, shining in the sun. We have views of lone houses on distant headlands, and of the church, with its bell arch, beside the road, with the Atlantic and the islands beyond.

After some scrubby land, we pass a small pond, with spike rush, flag iris and willow. Kinish Harbour, like a sea lake with its narrow mouth, is now seen. There are some pines on the right. Soon afterwards, we pass the entrance to a small estate of relatively new local authority houses; there are other houses, also, nearby.

(5) We come out opposite a sheltered lagoon, cut off from Kinish by a low wall, covered at high tide, . We turn left. Here, in the muffled silence of one misty March afternoon, we watched four pairs of mergansers courting on the millpond-still water two hundred yards from the road. Mergansers are amongst our loveliest ducks, rakish in appearance, with a crown like a wild crew-cut. Largely seafaring, they are sometimes seen close inshore. In courtship ritual, the black-headed males bob like clockwork toys, swell their breasts and throw their beaks skywards. The red headed females modestly cruise past.

Sycamores and alders arch over the road ahead and we pass through a dappled, leafy tunnel. This is a sheltered spot, with attractive houses and gardens half hidden behind escalonia hedges. In August, the verges beyond the 'tunnel' are bright with the brilliant orange of montbretia in flower. We ignore the road to the right, and continue south-west, direction Trá Bán.

Little Egret, a new bird to Ireland, now seen on the islands

We reach the church, with its three arched windows and bell arch above the gable. The crown of the macracarpa tree, in front of the house alongside, is planed flat by the wind. Now, on the roadside stone walls, lichen thrive, notably crispy lungwort and sea ivory, which has stiff, flat branches up to two inches long bearing reproductive nodules at the tips.

The road is straight and traffic-free. Behind Schull, to the north west, Mount Gabriel looms large against the sky; nearer true north, in the middle distance, a castle stands lonely on the mainland shore. Cape Clear Island comes into view ahead, with its signal tower. Trá Bán, the "white strand", a horseshoe-shaped sandy beach, is below us on the right. The islands to the north are Heir Island, the three Calfs, and beyond, Castle and Long, west of Schull.

The road divides in a Y. We follow the the right 'arm', a grassy track, past an old stone house and down towards the sea. Black rocks lie between us and Clear Island, which rises very high, with the signal tower and some houses silhouetted against the sky. With binoculars, we can see the road climbing the hill. On bright days, the sun reflects on the windows of the houses.

(6) We turn and retrace our steps. Now as we walk east towards the church, we see, in the middle distance, the sweep of West Bay to the north, with its two sandy beaches, enclosed by Drolain Point. The long, low buildings beyond the second beach are part of the Marine Station, housing libraries and high tech labs., reached by tracks across unshorn fields. Here, biologists study marine life, and the Sherkin Comment, with articles relating to the oceans of the world, is published quarterly. Unfortunately, the high cost of public liability insurance caused the close of the Station's sea aquarium, previously a great attraction.

(7) After passing the church, we take the road to the left, signposted Silver Strand. Stands of large sycamores and witch hazels edge the road. We shortly arrive at an 'isthmus', with Kinish Harbour on our right, a pebbly shore. At low tide, hardly a square foot of the muddy 'strand' of Kinish is without a worm cast. A cubic metre of healthy slob is said to contains more life than a cubic metre of Amazon rain forest; it's easy to believe it here, at Docknaganee. Now, a path across some small dunes, held together with marram, leads onto Silver Strand, a popular bathing beach in summer; the road alongside is white with wind-blown sand. Continuing, we pass a road to the left which leads to the Marine Station and an ancient promontory fort. The road straight ahead takes us to close views of Heir Island. There is no 'loop' route, so we must retrace our steps to the main road.

(8) At the main road, we turn left, heading for the pier and the ferry. The route back takes us, again, along the Kinish lagoon. Little egrets, a relatively new bird in Ireland (they first nested on the Blackwater in 1997 and since have colonised the south west coast) may be seen here, stalking the shallows; they are attractive, pure white herons, with black legs and yellow feet. There is a spinney of holly and Scots pine in a field on our right. We pass the new school, in modern pre-fab buildings, in front of the old school-house, neatly painted and well maintained. "Sherkin Male National School, 1892", says a plaque in front wall and at the rear, another plaque announces, "Sherkin Island Girls' and Boys' National School 1892 - 1992". Sacred Heart and Virgin Mary statutes can be seen through the windows. Can there be a lovelier spot for teaching or for learning? With the calm waters of Kinish on three sides, and banks of the "blossom'd furze" on the slopes opposite, the island master or mistress taught

Sherkin Friary

generations of pupils at this little school. While numbers have fallen off (Sherkin's population, now 100, was over 1,000 in the years before the Famine) at the time of writing, there are about a dozen children on the roll.

A house on a promontory over Kinish has a large yacht drawn up beside the garden; the harbour must be deep at high tides. We pass the Community Centre, and the library. A feature of this stretch in summer is puffing-and-panting holiday makers with their children and luggage rushing for the boat. Visitors tend to wait until the last minute. It is hard to leave Silver Strand, the island and its peace.

Below, on the left, we may see the ripples of the fat, slow mullet which come into Rugher Strand with each tide. Topping the rise, we head downhill towards the abbey and the pier. If we are early for the boat, we may divert to the pubs for post-amble drinks. Hospitable and relaxed, they both afford views of Baltimore and the approaching boat. At the pier, the children beg for "a last swim", don trunks and leap into the deep, clear water. Sometimes, in summer, the bay is full of mackerel as we cross, with white terns screaming and, further out, big, white, cruciform gannets, with black wing tips, diving on the shoals.

© Start point

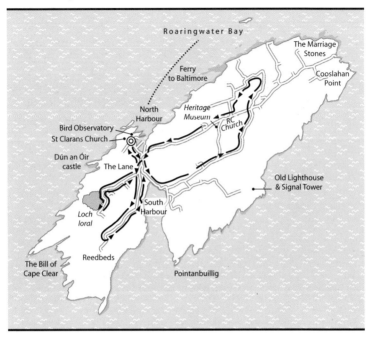

Roaringwater Bay

The Marriage Stones

Cooslahan Point

Ferry to Baltimore

North Harbour

Heritage Museum

RC Church

Bird Observatory

St Clarans Church

Dún an Óir castle

The Lane

Old Lighthouse & Signal Tower

South Harbour

Loch Ioral

The Bill of Cape Clear

Reedbeds

Pointanbuillig

Cape Clear Walk

Location, access and island life: Cape Clear Island, Oileán Chléire, (OS Sheet 88, centre at Square 9621) in Roaringwater Bay is 5km long and 3 km wide. Ferries cross from Baltimore. North Harbour, where the ferries dock, is 10km (6mls) south west of Baltimore. The island is a Gaeltacht, a thriving community speaking Irish and English with equal ease. The population, numbering 135, includes fishermen, farmers, artists and craftsmen, with holidaymakers arriving in summer. The pier is the hub; there are a couple of pubs, shops and craft outlets, and B&Bs, hostels and campsites nearby. Beyond it, the bohreens are as empty and unspoiled as any walker would wish for.

The walk, description and distance: The distance of our round is 6.5km (4 mls). The walk to Loch Ioral would add 4km.

Walking conditions: I have deliberately chosen the anti-clockwise route to avoid steep hills. The first part of the route is on surfaced roads. If we continue to Lough Ioral, we may need waterproof footwear.

An introduction.

Whatever the weather, the voyage to Oileán Chléire is likely to be exhilarating for the stranger. The Atlantic weather is so changeable that sunlight may be dancing on the water or salt spray blowing over the decks. In late summer, mackerel shoals often break the surface, and gannets rocket into the sea all around the boat. Cormorants and black guillemot are abundant. Dolphins are sometimes seen and whales migrate through these waters between June and December. Seals are common, and porpoises in summer.

The ferry passes between Sherkin and Cape Clear and affords great views of the empty end of Sherkin, and of Heir Island and the Calfs. We pass the Gascanane Rock; legend says that first-time visitors to Cléire should compose a verse in its honour to ensure a safe return to the mainland.

Itinerary.

(1) We start at the pier, a colourful scene with brightly-painted boats at anchor in the docks, and the relics of history all around us. Over centuries, Trá Chiaráin (St. Ciarán's Strand), as it is called, has seen the comings and goings of the islanders and their enterprises. An earlier name was Fionn Traigh Cleire (The Fair Strand of Cléire) and this may have given the island its name: 'clerus' possibly referred to 'clerk' or 'clergy', evidence of the island's ancient association with Christianity. St. Ciarán was born on Cléire in AD 352. Patrick did not arrive in Ireland until 432 , and, according to an old island saying, Patrick never came west of Leap (near Skibbereen), because the western people had already been Christianised by Ciarán and his brother Céim.

The ruined church of Cill Chiarán, to the right, is 12th century, possibly built on a church the saint raised himself. Nearby is a pillar stone, probably pre-Christian and indicating that the site was always sacred; crosses are carved into it, the stamp of the new faith. There is, also, a holy well, where pilgrims come to take water on Ciarán's Day, March 5th. He travelled far and wide, as has many a Cape Clear man, especially those who served in the navies and merchant fleets of Britain and the US. In Cornwall and Brittany, where he spread the faith, they observe the same Ciarán's Day, in his honour.

Further to the right is the Bird Observatory, venue of twitchers from all over the world. It was Ireland's first observatory, founded in 1959. Cape Clear, so far to the south, is often the first landfall for exhausted migrants. Rare avian vagrants regularly show up here, as do rare human ones in pursuit of 'ticks' and sightings.

(2) Leaving the pier, we pass signposts and a shop. We walk uphill, keeping right; we ignore the steep road going left to the church. After passing the memorial to those drowned in the Fastnet Yacht Race in 1979, we pass a pub, then a quaint old post box and an old stone house with quarry slates on the roof. A road goes right, signposted "Loch Ioral"; we ignore this – we will be walking it later. We pass a house with distinctive bollards in front,

The O'Driscoll Castle of Dún an Óir

then various houses, a pub and cottages. In August, the roadside and fields are splashed with the vivid orange with flowering montbretia. Hybridised in France as a garden exotic, it escaped from flower beds and, in Ireland, has added colour to the wild landscape. On Cape Clear, it is still in bloom in November. Furze, also called French gorse, is another Gallic import common in all the islands, useful, and colourful, for centuries. We pass a grotto, and a plaque to St. Ciarán.

Now sheltered South Harbour is ahead, with steep land rising on the other side. A seat and a pay-as-you-view telescope overlooks it and Thrush Glen, also called The Nordy Wood. The boggy ground supports goat willow, flag iris and spike rush. Heather, Irish dwarf gorse, bracken and montbretia colonises the white quartzite-type rock on the roadside cuttings. The water in harbour below is very blue and clear when the sun is shining.

Amongst the buildings on the shore is the Youth Hostel, once the home of the energetic Rev. Edward Spring, an Irish-speaking Kerryman whose personal mission was to convert the Roaringwater Bay islanders to the Reformed Church. During the Famine years, 1845-48, the soup he dispensed in Protestant schools and churches kept many a body and soul together during those terrible times, albeit they deserted him and returned to their own priests when the emergency passed. Ahead of his time, he

26

established a school which taught through the medium of Irish. Despite his sincere efforts, the Church of Ireland had a short life, on the island. The congregation was so small that it was soon closed, and the cut stone sold to build a bank in Schull.

There is a picnic table beside the pebbly beach; it is a pleasant place to pause and take in the scene. Further along the beach, is the old Telegraph Station, set up in the 1860s. As liners from the US passed, a boat would be rowed out to collect sealed containers thrown overboard with the latest news from America; this would then be cabled forward, ahead of the liner's arrival in the UK. Thus, the humble people of Oileán Chléire were the first Europeans to know of the American Civil War and the assassination of Abraham Lincoln. At the corner of the station, a road goes left to the old lighthouse; along it are many excellent bird-watching sites, gardens where the migrants find cover in which to rest after their exhausting journeys.

(3) We take the first road left, beside a house with cabbage palms in the garden just beyond the Millennium Wall, and go uphill to pass the National School; the original building dates from 1897. There is a solar panel in the roof and, presumably, the pupils don't each have to bring a sod of turf to school on winter days, as was the tradition in many country schools of yore. A stream passes under the school yard and comes out in a small waterfall. The verges and road side walls support a wealth of ferns and wild flowers, harts tongue ferns and primroses in April, foxgloves and wall pennywort in June, pink fuchsia in September. Watercress grows in the ditches. Lichens thrive on the stone walls, predominantly the grey lecanora species. There are clumps of pines, here and there.

A big Monterey pine outside a farmhouse on the left is spectacularly sculpted by the prevailing winds; the need for shelter is evidenced by the stone walls and escalonia around the house. Looking back, we see a pattern of green fields between fields colonised by bracken, once cultivated as bedding for humans and animals. The nearby landscape is heath land. A stone stile on the left leads across the Cnoicín, the little hill, to the island church on the dorsal road. For walkers wanting a shorter return to the pier, this 'mountain path', Casán an tSléibhe, will be useful. We will continue on the road but a short stroll up this path is well worth while; we pass through another stile, through bracken and past woods of alder (with catkins and cones on the trees in autumn), sitka spruce and lodgepole; the views from the high ground are panoramic, over South Harbour and out to the Fastnet Rock, with the old lighthouse silhouetted against the sky to the south and the Calf Islands low on the sea to the north. It is truly lovely to see the flowering heather mixed in with gorse, and the path is a testament to the value the islanders' place on their natural heritage.

Loch Ioral, where stones near the shore may mark old flax ponds

Back on the road, we see the way ahead rising to a hill and going through a gap. A roadside plaque with the words "Chrathach Thiar", refers to a standing stone – a gallán – in a field on the right; markings on it may be in the Celtic ogham alphabet. So pale are the lichens on the field walls – made of stones cleared from the land, and thus fulfilling two purposes – that one might think they are whitewashed.

We have views of the old lighthouse and the Signal Tower to the right; these can be reached by the lower road at South Harbour. The lighthouse, built of granite shipped from Cornwall, was in use until 1854. However, located almost 500 ft above the sea, it was often blanketed in fog or low cloud and many an ill-fated mariner, rounding the Mizen, stayed too close to shore, leading to shipwreck on the Calfs, Cape Clear itself or Sherkin. This was the fate of the "Stephen Whitney", an American liner which foundered on the West Calf with the loss of 90 lives in 1847. The outcry led to the building of the first Fastnet Lighthouse in 1854, and the decommissioning of the Clear island light. Signal Towers were built along the Irish coast in the immediate aftermath of the attempted French invasion of 1798 (see Heir Island Walk).

At the top of the rise, is the island playing field. The two wind turbines on the hill, the highest point of the island, 533ft, 161.5m. are no longer in use since an under-sea electricity cable was laid to the island in 1997. There are panoramic views ahead to Baltimore and, to the north, Mount Gabriel, with its twin communications "golf balls" on the summit.

We reach Tobar na gCeann, the Well of the Head, where a stone plaque, beautifully carved in the old Irish lettering, provides a roadside homily: "Christ said that he who drinks the water I give to him will never again thirst". The well likely dates from long before the Christian era.

There is a fine farmhouse in view, with three chimneys, a classic rural home with nothing added, no verandahs, porches or peaky dormers. Dead plain, with nice proportions of windows and door, and a lean-to at the end, also slated, of field stone, it demonstrates the triumph of grace over ornament. Down to left is an example of a sensitively-converted farmhouse, showing how it should be done, if it must be done. Previously, this was a famous pub, The Rising Sun (Éirí na Gréine), and is now a hostel for students coming to study the Irish language on Cape Clear.

The Marriage Stones. Couples who join hands through the stone remain joined forever.

(4) At An Chrois, the four-cross road, we go straight ahead, down towards the sea. The small green fields are a joy to behold. We can see the Trá Bán, the White Strand, on Sherkin, with the Marine Station. To the left of Sherkin is Heir, and then Calf East.

As we swing around, with the turn of the road, Mizen is ahead, far away, and the hills around it. Sheemon Point Lighthouse, at the entrance to Crookhaven, can be seen with binoculars.

The road goes steeply downhill, grass growing up the middle. Ahead there is a rough bohreen going down to the sea but we turn sharp left, going west. There are good-looking houses along the way, mostly old farmhouses with a fresh coat of paint and nothing fiddley added. Neither did the 1960s 'bungalow blitz' of scattered shoebox houses spoil the beauty of the landscape here, as elsewhere in Ireland.

This is a lovely, winding country road, with grass down the middle, and swathes of montbretia, bright orange in August. A donkey grazes contentedly in a briary field. We pass, on the right, an abalone farm; abalones are Californian shellfish, somewhat like oysters. Soon after, a sign indicates Cnocán na mBáirneach, the Small Hill of the Limpets. Limpets have conical shells and cling to seashore rocks, which they graze, like cows. Mistakenly called barnacles, one Irish variety is tough as old boots but another is a close relative of the 'lapas' so highly regarded in Spain. During the Great Famine of 1845-47, shellfish, probably including limpets, helped sustain the island people. We pass the house of Concubar Ó Siocháin, author of the classic Seanchas Chléire (The Man from Clear Island), now out of print but by far the finest book ever written about the island.

Beyond the Calf Islands, with ruins on the westernmost Calf, we can see the beacon on Long Island. Now, a pleasant bohreen on the right goes down to the biggest beach on the island, a five minute diversion and a fine place for a cooling dip on a summer day. Back on the main route, we take the cul-de-sac road going west, and turn left, uphill, towards the church. At the T-junction, we are back on the dorsal road, and we go right, towards the church. This was built, in 1839, on the site of an older church, which had a thatched roof and was said to be 'as destitute of ornament as any barn'. The present church is also a plain and unfussy place of worship, with an aura of sanctity and peace. The path mentioned earlier, Casán an tSléibhe, across the island, emerges in a neat stile by the western gable.

Beyond the church, is the Heritage Centre, until 1897, a National School for girls. It houses many items of interest in the long history of Oileán Chléire, with a collection of 1,500 photographs by Michael Minihane of the Irish Examiner, Pierce Hickey and other photographers. It is open daily through June, July and August, and otherwise a key is available at the Library or on the island bus. Various artefacts, including a quern stone for grinding grain, are exhibited outside.

On the right, is a goat farm, and a cottage shop where cheese, yoghurt, ice-cream and other goat milk produce is for sale. The owner is English and has been resident on the island for many years. Wayside plaques tell us about the lighthouse, off to the south, and we have magnificent views of the Fastnet on the horizon, four miles away, and of the whole western end of the island, with a ruined castle midway along the north west shore. This is Dún an Óir, 'the fort of gold', one of the last castles left to Fineen O Driscoll, 'the Rover'. Sir Fineen, as he was for a while, supported the doomed Irish-Spanish cause at Kinsale in 1601. He lost his lands for his trouble and died destitute in his castle at Lough Hyne. After the Kinsale defeat, Captain Richard Tyrell took refuge at Dún an Óir and the castle was bombarded by English cannons, hauled from the ships to the hill above it. Thus, the land side is in ruins, while the sea side is unscathed but for the toll of time and weather. Acres of bracken have subsumed the fallen walls.

Flag Iris, brilliant yellow, flowering in wet land in May and June

This is a lovely route downhill, the views opening before us. We can see both sides of the island and have a birds-eye view of the little port below; it would be steep going if we were doing this walk the other way around. St. Ciarán is said to have been born near here in AD 352; his birth is recorded in the Annals of Innisfallen, written in the 11th century at an island monastery in Lough Leane, in Killarney.

(5) We reach the junction over the harbour; the road down to the pier is on our right. To continue to Loch Ioral, we keep left, walking uphill, passing a craft shop and pub. After a short distance, the road divides at a house with distinctive bollards in front. We keep right, and pass a B&B and a line of cottages. Now, the path again divides, and a sign indicates Lough Ioral up a steep road to the right. We can now continue straight ahead to Loch Ioral, and return by the same route. However, if we are to follow 'the bird watchers' loop' (see conditions at paragraph (6) below) we ignore this and take the sign indicating a camping ground to the left. We shortly pass this camp site, beautifully situated above South Harbour.

Over the fields to the right, in a house now gone but for a single gable wall, the Timoleague Chalice was discovered by a priest saying a 'station' mass at the dwelling in 1851. He spotted an old box and asked about its history. The man of the house said that, many years before, some of his family had found an open boat adrift at sea, with two men dead, and one alive, all friars, aboard it. They rescued the living man, and buried the dead. Before the surviving friar left the island, he entrusted them with the box, which they had not opened to that day. Now, with the priest on hand, it was opened, and a gold chalice found inside, with a Latin inscription identifying it as belonging to the Franciscan Abbey at Timoleague, on Courtmacsherry Bay, in West Cork. In 1642, Cromwellian soldiers attacked the Timoleague Castle and failing to take it, burnt the abbey. It would seem the three friars made their escape, with the Abbey's greatest treasure, in an open boat and drifted west until they were found off Clear Island. The chalice was returned to Timoleague, having rested 200 years in an island home, surely a testament to the good faith and trustworthiness of the Cape Clear people.

Streams run down to the left off the road, marked by lines of sallies and goat willow; their supple branches were used for weaving lobster pots in the past. As we progress, we find sea ivory lichen on the walls; somewhere I've read that it's called Neptune's Beard; it's wiry, grey and grows not far from the sea. The road is less well kept than others; it peters out at a dead end. A couple of old routes are barred, with signs "Beware of the Bull".

The island ferry seen through a window of Cill Chiarán church.

Ahead, we see an upright stone on a small hill, silhouetted against the sky; this is the last man standing of the False Men, false lookouts erected by the English to deter a French landing during Napoleonic times. Bog land, safe refuge for migrant birds, lies before it. The 'carnivorous' insect-trapping plants, sundew and butterwort, are found here and bright-yellow flag irises shoot tall and showy above the reedy grass in May.

We reach 'the last house' and the road becomes a track. There is an extensive reed bed to our left, with tall, purple-headed reeds in flower late summer. They move gracefully when there is a breeze sweeping across them, and myriad swallows and martins sometimes gather here in Autumn, perhaps to fatten up on the abundant insect life before heading south, almost to the tip of Africa, on their epic journeys.

(6) Ahead is a small wooden stile. A sign says, "Beware of the Bull", but a trodden path continues across the field. The walker must make up his or her own mind what to do next; the author cannot recommend trespassing or taking chances with bulls. Advice may be sought from the Tourist Info Office, Cape Clear Co-op and Enterprise Centre near the Bird Observatory at North Harbour. For myself, I walked the route with a couple of regular birders who said the owner did not object so long as they closed the gates and did not disturb his animals; nevertheless, it is best to check. Needless to say, we did not bring a dog.

Having ensured that the landowner does not object, we follow the trodden path across muddy ground and reach a broad ditch. The best course is to stay well in to the field centre until a gap between the stone walls become evident, where the ditch can be crossed. The land is rough with another reed bed below to the left. Western Marsh orchid may be found in the wet ground, flowering in May and June; it does not occur in Britain. We see a house ahead, and come to a gate, then another gate, which carries a "Beware of the Bull" sign. The house is substantial, with a neat garden, and chickens pecking away on the lawn, a very peaceful, old fashioned scene.

We now walk the tarred road along the eastern shore of Loch Ioral. There are stands of reeds and, in summer, a dense floating mat of amphibious bistort makes a red band in the shallows along the south end. Mallard duck are common, and nest here. Black-headed gulls bob on the open water, and herons are often seen, standing with their wings behind their backs, like Sandeman sherry ads, in the shallows; perhaps they are hunting the small, black leeches which, along with amphipod crustacea, are the main lake fauna. Attempts to seed Ioral with trout and other fish have failed; either the water is too alkaline or it become eutrophic and airless in warm summers and the fish die. In the north-west corner and on the southern shore, stones laid out into the water indicate old flax pools, used to soak and rot away the outer stalk of flax stems, exposing the fibres used in linen manufacture.

As we go steeply downhill towards the harbour and the pier, we can turn to enjoy fine views of the Fastnet on the horizon, especially dramatic as the sun sinks into the sea.

◎ Start point

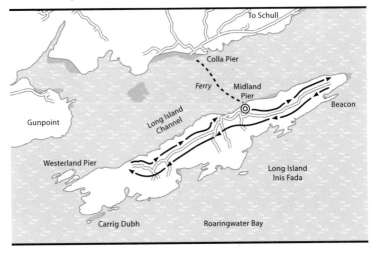

To Schull

Colla Pier

Ferry

Midland Pier

Gunpoint

Long Island Channel

Beacon

Westerland Pier

Long Island Inis Fada

Carrig Dubh

Roaringwater Bay

Long Island Walk

Location, access and island life: Long Island, Inis Fada, (OS Sheet 88, centre at square 9128), is located on the north side of Roaringwater Bay, opposite the townland of Colla, three kilometres south of Schull on the road following the coast. The island population numbers ten but some of the cottages have been renovated and attract visitors in summer. The ferry to Long Island leaves from Colla Pier; the passage takes only ten minutes. The island is 4km (2.3 mls) long, by less than a kilometre wide.

The walk, description and distance: No loop walk is available on Long. We walk as far east as we can go, then turn and walk back as far west. On each leg, there are views and perspectives on the return that we didn't see on the outward. The total distance is about 6.5km, or 4 miles.

Walking conditions: The going is easy, most of it on tarred road, but off-road can be boggy so waterproof footwear is advised.

An introduction.

Schull is a West Cork holiday town favoured by Dublin 4 visitors, yachtsmen who launch and ladies who lunch. *Inis Fada*, Long Island, is only a few miles down the road but it is a universe away. At Colla Pier, in view of the island, holidaymakers bathe, mess about in small boats and troll for mackerel from the rocks in summer. Colla serves Midland Pier, across the channel, and the two townlands have long been connected. At one time, farmers swam cattle back and forth behind their boats.

As we cross the sound, we might reflect that here, in December, 1795, a brig en route from Cadiz to Dublin with a cargo of Christmas oranges foundered and was attacked by the industrious citizens with axes so that "not an atom was left afloat". Oranges and timber from Long Island were sold all over West Cork. In 1838, a bullion ship broke up nearby, spilling priceless cargo, including seven silver plates, weighing a hundredweight each, onto the sea bed, keeping divers at work for eight years.

In the 1940s, a local man devised a small unmanned, self-steering sailboat that could carry light goods to and from the island. In another island initiative, in 1973 the Long Island Carriage Service printed its own postage stamps, issuing some 60,000 sets before the National Post Office had publication banned.

On the coast ahead is Cuas an Mhuillin, a small inlet, with a rock behind it from which 'curative water' is said to issue. People come from all over County Cork to collect it. Also, near Midland Pier, half way between the small beach and the rock platforms, there is a deep cave. It runs a distance into the island, far beyond the reach of natural light. John Shelley, the ferryman, might point it out. Clearly, care should be taken not to enter it when the tide is rising. When researching tidal waves around the Irish coast in the wake of the tragic tsunami in South East Asia in December 2004, I was told of a massive wave that carried a man off from Westerland strand on Long Island in the 1940s. Lewis' *Cork* (1837) says "...it is traditionally stated that, in 830, such a violent tempest occurred that the sea broke over the island and forced it asunder in three parts.."

Itinerary.

(1) After disembarking at Midland Pier, we follow the road left to walk to the island's easternmost point and the beacon looking out on Castle Island. We then retrace our steps to Midland and walk west as far as we can go, past a settlement with some picturesque ruins to a small beach and Westerland Pier. No loop walk is available on Long, but there are views and perspectives on the way back that one didn't see on the outward leg.

As we set off from the pier, gulls hang low over the road, riding an up-draught and crying out as if outraged by our arrival. There is no other living thing to be seen. We pass a few small, neat houses, all of the same design, even to the extensions which have sometimes been added. Some are freshly whitewashed, and look newly built. In fact, they are examples of a type of slate roofed house built by the Congested Districts Board on many of the Irish islands in 1928; the old houses had sod roofs. Twenty six such dwellings were built on Long. Some have been renovated as holiday homes. Families with a dozen children or more once lived in them.

The harvest of the sea was often the mainstay of the islanders

The island population may have numbered three hundred people in the nineteenth century; now, it numbers ten. In 1871, fifteen years after the great potato famine had decimated the people of West Cork, forty houses were still occupied; now, only six of these families still keep a foothold. Long Islanders were a hardy people; the men were fishermen and farmers. Their wives were mighty oarswomen, rowing fifteen miles to Skibbereen to the mill.

Grass grows up the middle of the narrow, which swings around to the right before running more or less straight down the backbone of the island. Irish dwarf gorse has colonised the rocky fields, and the stone walls are colonised with wall pennywort, with flower stalks like miniature, white foxgloves, and stonecrop, a succulent that puts out small white flowers in July. We also meet the usual foreign colonists - originally 'escapes' from (probably mainland) gardens - montbretia, from France, flowering flame-red in July and August, and fuchsia, originally from Chile but now naturalised all over Ireland's south west. Fuchsia is ubiquitous enough to have an Irish name, Deora Dé, meaning God's Tears, possibly associating the bright red flowers with Christ crucified. It is used as a shelter belt around some of the isolated houses.

But for wheel tracks by the ditches, the narrow road would be a long field. Here and there, we come upon cars which are not in the best of condition; in fact, some seem to have been immobile for years. No doubt, one day the big breaker-truck will come and take them to the great scrap yard on the mainland. Meanwhile, they moulder in ditches, while the vegetation all around grows up, and through, them. Enthusiasts might find original parts for long obsolete models.

In July and August, the land between us and the sea is gold with gorse and purple with heather. There is not a soul to be seen. From a field on the right, white cattle idly watch us as we pass. The air is full of bee-buzz and bird song; swallows spin in the sky overhead, and skim over the bracken. A leisurely heron rises like a wind-blown umbrella from a nearby hill - an unusual roost for a heron - and a pair of unleisurely snipe rocket from a roadside wetland and zig-zag into the sky. They are quite out of synch with the peace of Long Island, but instinct prevails.

Stonechats flit from briar to briar and a cock linnet, with the red breast of summer plumage, sings from a post. Yellow flag stand tall and bright in a marshy field

(2) As we pass through a cutting and ascend to higher ground, the views are magnificent, Clear Island to the south, Sherkin, seen over the low-lying Calf Islands, to the south east, then Baltimore town, with the Napoleonic-era Signal Tower on the hills above. In the sea far to the west, the Fastnet Rock and its lighthouse, stands lonely and shining in the sun. In Irish, it is called Charraig Aonair, the 'lone rock', surely more appropriate than Fastnet, although it was so named on Italian maps of the late medieval times. The fence posts and roadside stone walls are botanical gardens of lichens. Shortly, we pass a ruin resplendent with orange xanatoria. The West Cork people are fearless with paint when it comes to their houses but, in the case of this ruin, time and nature may conspire to eclipse their most imaginative efforts. A lichen associated with the shore, sea ivory, like wisps of stiff, grey-green hair, also thrives on Long Island stones.

The beacon at the end of Long Island, marking the entrance to Schull Harbour can be seen ahead. In the island peace, cars catching the sunlight as they pass along the Colla road seem like phenomena in another world, travelling in another time, and the huge communication domes shining atop Mount Gabriel are artefacts on another planet. It is easy to forget not just the bistros, book shops and boutiques of Schull, but the entire island of Ireland. Inis Fada, for all that it is measures less than three miles by a half mile wide, becomes much larger than its giant neighbour, which is remote and unreal; the things that happen there do not happen here.

A cormorant, familiar on the coast, hanging its wings out to dry

We come upon a tall post fixed upright in the ditch on the right side of the road, riddled with holes which might have been made by ship worms, or teredo worms (perhaps it was sea wrack, or salvage?) and with a large carbuncle or knot three quarters way up; it is a dramatic piece of natural sculpture. Opposite, beyond some marshy fields, is an upright stone, perhaps an ancient Standing Stone or perhaps simply a scratching post for cattle; there is no one to ask.

(3) As we approach the beacon, the road narrows to a lane, overgrown, and muddy in wet weather. At the time of writing, there is a "Duty of Care" notice on an entrance, indicating that the land beyond is private. Locals have told me that they themselves and visitors have always walked out to the beacon. If they crossed private land, apparently the owners saw no reason to stop them. In the 1990s and early 2000s, however, landowners were concerned about personal injury claims by trespassers, but the Occupiers Liability Act 1995 was finally proved to indemnify them against such claims by a Supreme Court Ruling in January 2005. In the light of this reassurance, the notice may well be removed.

We walk over trackless, open ground just above the rock platforms which are covered with impressive lichens. There are fallen walls and loose rocks here and there, and a small pond below us, edged by luxuriant royal fern, our most majestic native fern, sometimes achieving heights of 4m. We are looking out at Castle Island. Here, tenants were savagely evicted and their houses torn down in an infamous action by a landlord called Marmion in 1890. There is no trace of them now, only a few stones on stones.

We cross a stream above a small, sheltered cove, and continue through a stile, which looks like a sheep gap, onto a field above. Below us, a large, black rock lies offshore across a channel of water as clear as an aquarium, a pristine marine environment, with shellfish and anemones, and long, brown eel grass moving in the flow. Between us and Clear Island, the three Calf Islands lie low on the sea, with ruins of houses visible. Settlements survived on the Calfs until the mid 20th century, despite the inhospitality of the location, often cut off for weeks in winter storms. One day, as we paused to enjoy the view, a small flock of golden plover suddenly descended on the rocks like a fall of leaves, stayed a few minutes and then took flight again, underwings flashing white as they turned. A large grey seal poked its nose over the still surface of the cove to look at us. We whistled and, as is usual with seals, it swam closer and gazed at us, full of curiosity.

Pink tussocks of sea thrift brighten the black rocks in June. From the beacon, we can see the ruined O'Mahony tower house at the eastern end Castle Island. It stands on a promontory over the main landing place, probably on the site of an earlier fort.

Walking the roads of Long

(4) Retracing our steps, we pass Midland Pier and turn left for Westerland, on what our ferryman describes as "a nice tidy *slachtmhar* walk, where you can keep your shoes clean..."

At the time of writing, we pass some ruined houses, and an old pump on the right; the handle works but no water arrives. The road climbs slightly uphill and past a hundred metres of exposed rock faces which, for a student of lichens, would provide hours of interest. Stonecrop, maiden hair spleenwort and black spleenwort are amongst the many plants that colonise the rocks, and one October, I found beautiful waxcaps mushrooms, orange and vivid red, growing up amongst the mosses. I believe they were *Hygrocybe punicea*, 'punicea' meaning 'of pomegranates' or 'garnet red'. I have also found orange and red waxcaps on Clear Island; these were, I think, *Hygrocybe coccinea*, called Scarlet Hood, and equally vivid.

A linnet. The cock has a deep red breast in spring. They are strong, sweet singers.

We pass the island school, now converted to a dwelling, and we can see Coney Island to the right, not far offshore, with a nice house on it and a pretty cove. There are some green fields ahead, to right and left of the road as it goes down into a dip. When we reach the rise beyond, we see, the Goat Islands, high out of the water.

Across the sound, on our right, Mount Gabriel is large against the sky, with the cleft of Barnancleeve Gap on its right shoulder. Four thousand year ago, paths crossed the mountain to reach the workings on its slopes, the first copper mines in Western Europe. These paths are long since subsumed beneath the brown blanket of bog but, without doubt, the gap would have been one the routes. Nowadays, it carries the road from Schull to Durrus and from here, so far away, we can see the windscreens of cars going through it flashing in the sun.

(5) We now approach the houses clustered above Westerland Pier, about fifteen in all, many in ruins. The views are very beautiful, and dramatic. A steep-sided channel separates the two Goat Islands, with a tower on Goat Island Little, on the left. The steep-sided channel between them is a dramatic sight.

We reach a T-junction, and the land ahead is uncultivated, rock-rent and bockety, with more gorse than grazing. What appear to be two low towers are silhouetted against the western sea; they are the ruined gables of long-abandoned houses. Around them relics of old potato ridges extend down to the very rocks of the shore. This land offered little sustenance, and that little hard won. Of food for the spirit, there was a feast, and if the native people could have lived on the scenery, their bellies would have indeed been filled. Here, like the sea or sky, the land is nature's domain and humans pass but leave little trace of their having been. The moorland and bog stretches like a brown mantle to the sea: in winter, it is as drab as sackcloth, in summer, purple with heather and golden with gorse. The ferryman said Westerland was a place of great spiritual force, and it is not

A fine bull calf. On Long, there are patches of rich pasture

hard to believe him. There is a power and majesty in the empty land, the sea and sky, and Ireland seems a smaller place, close by but infinitely remote.

We turn right, down to the beach, and Westerland Pier. The small strand is a lonely, but lovely place, and some rare plants colonise the shingle. The horned poppy is one; its bright yellow flowers may be found as late as October. Little Robin, a member of the geranium family, also grows here. It is very like the often-seen Herb Robert but taller and greener and with smaller flowers. It is very rare, present elsewhere in Ireland only on old walls around Cork city. John Akeroyd's book of island flora says it may not be an Irish native and, in the case of Long, may have been introduced a very long time ago. It sometimes grows almost prostrate along the shingle.

Looking out over the land, where any trace of fields has long been subsumed by furze and heather, there is not a single human artefact to snare one in time. A few hours walking on Long is like a holiday from the world and its business. One wonders if one ever wants to set foot on the mainland again.

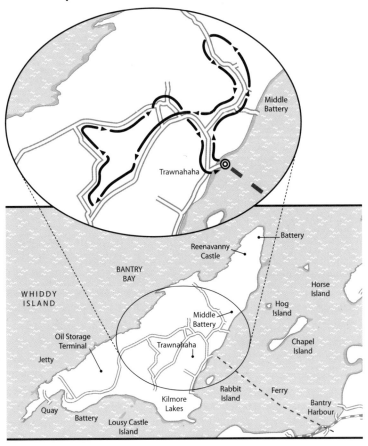

47

Whiddy Island Walk

Location, access and island life: Whiddy Island (OS Sheet 85, starting point at GR 970495) is at the eastern end of Bantry Bay. A ferry plies regularly from the pier on the N71 road entering Bantry from the south. It takes twelve minutes to cross the three kilometres of water to Whiddy Island. Lewis, in his survey of Cork in 1831, noted that the island was three miles (5km) long and average of one mile (1.6km) wide, with 1,218 statute acres of excellent land and 714 inhabitants. Today, the island residents number about 16. Crops are no longer widely sown and some of the land is rented out for grazing to 'off-islanders'. Many outsiders daily come to work at the Terminal, so the ferry can be busy mornings and evenings. Some holiday cottages are available for rent.

The walk, description and distance: A walk of approx. 6km (4mls) with spurs to north and east, and a loop towards the centre of the island. The views of the harbour of Glengarriff and the huge Caha Mountains on the Beara Peninsula are unsurpassed.

Walking conditions: We stay largely on bohreens and roads, so good walking shoes will suffice. Binoculars are invaluable on this walk.

An introduction.

The vast inlet of Bantry Bay is 34km (21mls) long and 10km (6 mls) wide at the mouth, narrowing to 3km. In 1796, the Irish rebel, Theobald Wolfe Tone, Protestant landowner and founder of The United Irishmen, arrived here with a French fleet, carrying 15,000 troops. Vile weather and bad seamanship prevented a landing, and the fleet returned in disarray to France. However, two years later, coinciding with the Rising of 1798, he arrived in Lough Swilly, in Donegal, with a French force of 5,000, where he was engaged and defeated by a British fleet. He was captured, transferred to Dublin, tried for treason and executed. His statue stands in the square named after him in Bantry town.

Bantry Bay is one of Europe's largest and best natural harbours. It has always been favoured with trade, and in 1961, because of the deep water anchorage afforded, an oil terminal was established at its western end, with giant super-tankers anchoring close offshore. The eastern end of the island, nearest Bantry town, remains unspoiled, with green, rolling hills, good pastures, some wild habitat, and small, sandy coves.

Itinerary.
(1) The ferry quay on Whiddy is substantial. The only island hostelry, The Bank House, stands above it; it is normally open during the summer months. Below the garden, are weedy rocks and tide pools with an abundance of rock-pool fish and other marine life. The five small islands nearby, including Rabbit Island, the nearest, provide great protection from the weather and the anchorage here is reckoned to be the safest in the bay, with a depth of five or six fathoms at low tide. From the pub garden, the mirror-calm water and the moored boats present an almost picture-postcard scene.

We set off up a narrow road with a fuchsia hedge on the right, and the pub apple tree behind it. At the T-junction, we turn right (the sign says Bantry Terminals). The field on the left is resplendent with the yellow blooms of flag iris in June. The local townland has the interesting name of Trawnahaha. It sounds straight out of Longfellow's Hiawatha; in fact, it comes from the Irish for 'the strand of the bridge, Trá na Átha'. We have a lexicon of beautiful and romantic place names in Ireland, the old Gaelic names. Look at any OS map; there is Lisheenaleen, Coomanore, Shandrum, Coolboy, Reenavanny. There are hundreds on a single sheet; they are in every parish. They are our names for places. They have meaning; they are not, like the Anglicised versions, simply sounds.

Opposite this vernacular field of yellow flags, is a children's playground and a concrete mini-golf course; it is, indeed, a holy and wholesome thought to provide some amenity for the children and the visitors. As we proceed, we look out, over marshy fields, at the mussel-lines strung across the waters of inner Bantry Bay. At times, the mussel-lines have been a contentious issue; tourist interests and fishermen have objected on the grounds of scenic detriment and obstruction of free passage. And ecologists have worried about the detritus on the sea floor. But, others applaud the initiative, in a time when the future of wild fish and all seafood stocks are threatened.

The ferry quay at Whiddy, sheltered by Rabbit Island.

Over the back of Chapel Island, and far behind the bay shores, we see Knockboy (An Cnoc Buí, the yellow mountain), rising to 706m, part of the Shehy Mountain range. Reed beds edge the marshy roadside fields. In late October, we find honeysuckle, and trefoil still in flower. A feature of Whiddy is that many plants continue flowering late into the year, late even for West Cork, which is often later than elsewhere in Ireland.

(2) We turn right, opposite the green-painted letter box and walk down a narrow road with grass growing up the middle, montbretia on the ditches and native bushes of blackthorn, hazel, whitethorn and holly along the sides. We can see it climbing gently ahead of us. In Autumn, there are blackberries and sloes on the bushes. It would be interesting to count the shrub species in each thirty yards of length and apply Hopper's Hypothesis to work out the age of the hedge; there would be one species for every 100 years it has existed. Wet ground on the left supports abundant goat willow. The ferns are harts tongue and lady fern and there is much bracken.

We pass a white farmhouse with traditional tin roofed barns, painted green and well-maintained, and the ruins of an older residence nearby. We see big mountains off to our left, on the other side of Bantry Bay, blue, misty peaks rising further and further back, the Caha Mountains and the borders of Kerry. The laneway is sheltered, with celandine, dog violets and primroses in early spring and, later, foxgloves and meadowsweet. In the island silence, the hum of the foraging bees seems louder than ashore.

A ruined house on the right turns out to be the Whiddy Island National School, built in 1887. The gate is framed in fuchsia (which, of course, originates in Chile) but a more sinister alien, Japanese knotweed, has invaded the yard and the roadside. Passing here, we have more than once heard the plaintiff calls of curlews flying overhead, a haunting sound somehow appropriate to the abandoned school yard which once, no doubt, rang with the sounds of children at play.

(3) A small, green lane runs down to the sea and a boat slip opposite uninhabited Chapel Island. From here, when the tide is down, one can work one's way along the beach to the site of an American sea plane terminal dating from World War I. Sea planes were stationed here to search out German submarines on the convoy routes to and from America along Ireland's south-west coast. Not much remains, only concrete aprons, and some water tanks.

Whiddy National School, 1887.

A short distance beyond the lane, a gate to the right of the road, with the signs 'Beware of Bull' and 'Private Property' at the time of writing, leads to a field which one must cross to reach the Middle Battery. The gate piers of the original track up which, no doubt, men were marched and cannon were hauled, can still be seen close by. The field belongs to a local farmer who told me he would not object to walkers crossing it, but it would be best if they asked, in case there was a bull. I understand that the Battery is currently owned by a Belgian national, resident overseas, and presumably he cannot be asked. I must leave it to walkers to make their own decision about visiting the site. There are hopes that arrangements for public access to this interesting item of built heritage can be made to everyone's satisfaction before long.

There are three gun batteries on Whiddy. All are more or less the same in layout, but Middle Battery is the largest. Built on high ground, the redoubt was completed in 1806 in response to the incursion of a French fleet into Bantry Bay in 1796.

The barracks, still extant, housed some seven officers, one hundred and eighty eight men and twelve guns. It was defended by a circular fosse or dyke, 8.5m wide and 10m deep, inside which a parapet wall, with gun emplacements, enclosed a level circular area of diameter 68m. At centre, are three rectangular rows of single storey barracks, all with barrel vaulted ceilings and originally with hipped slate roofs.

The North East Battery (1807), now inaccessible, was of smaller diameter (58m) as was the West Battery (1808) at Reenaknock, at the centre of which is a fortified tower. Both housed 100 men and 8 guns. Clearly, the English greatly feared a landing by the French and a country-wide uprising by the Irish. In 1689, twenty French ships had fought a running battle with an English fleet between Bere Island (ibid.) and Dursey (ibid.) and French troops were landed, while 1796 had seen an attempted French invasion, led by United Irishman, Theobald Wolfe Tone, with 40 French ships carrying a force of 15,000 men. Some French troops were landed on Bere Island but the expedition failed, storms, not the English, scattering the fleet.

The fosse is now colonised by large sycamore trees, elders, whitethorns, blackthorns and willows and a variety of attractive ferns thrive in its deep, sheltered ravine. A bridge of railway sleepers crosses it on the eastern side and enters the compound. From the same side, the views over Chapel Island and the bay are impressive. Hydrangeas and other flowers gone wild are relics of the old gardens while the massive walls, up to ten feet thick, and their impressive brick facings, are colonised by spleenwort, toadflax, wall pennywort and many banded snails, the ancestors of which must have been here long before the buildings, in fact before Whiddy was an island at all. The corridor between the barrack buildings is overgrown with montbretia, a hybrid French creation thriving in Ireland since it escaped from gardens, flowering vivid orange in August, like heads of wild, red hair.

Garden shrubs and bushes, gone wild, surround an old iron pump, and there are iron posts marked with red, perhaps to do with old gun emplacements.

The Middle Battery. The officers' quarters.

Entrants should here proceed with care, for fear of open wells or pits. Circling the barracks, along the parapets, the view is 360 degrees of spectacular scenery with vistas that include, to the west, the Caha Mountains and the distant peaks of Kerry, Glengarriff Harbour and Garinish Island, and Bantry House and estate to the east.

On the north end of the island, the ruins of Reenavanny Castle may be seen, and beyond it, the inaccessible North East Battery; binoculars will give us an excellent long-distance view. The landscape is particularly striking in Autumn light, when the bracken has died back and reddened, and there is still a dash of red fuchsia and yellow gorse here and there. The 'castle' is a tower house of the O'Sullivan Beres. Built in the reign of Henry VI (1422-1461), it stands on a rock outcrop. It was occupied by Carew, Lord President of Munster, during the reign of Elizabeth I, and was destroyed by Ireton during the English Civil War of 17th century. Much of it collapsed during gales in 1920 and now only the south west side remains. The castle can be reached by trekking over the rough land.

(4) The road below the Middle Battery continues west. We descend a slope and pass a fine traditional farmhouse, with only the windows changed. In October, fat black elder berries catch the sun light on a tree opposite. The road twists and turns. If we look to the right, through a gap in the bushes we can again see, through binoculars, the low stump of Reenavanny Castle.

The quietness, the entire absence of traffic and the magnificence of the Caha Mountains across the broad expanse of sea are intriguing features of this sector. We arrive at a field gate, and the roadway beyond is gravelled, leading to a private house. This is as far as we can go east unless we secure permission to cross fields and ditches. We will return to the post box and follow the bohreens going west from there.

(5) Arriving at the post box, we turn right. Foxgloves, in bloom in June, line the road side. We pass some houses, and two right turnings, the second signposted for Bantry terminals - opposite, stands a fine crab apple tree (the name 'crab' comes from 'scrab', the old Norse word for 'scrubby'). We ignore both turnings and continue on the straight road south-west.

We pass a farmhouse with chickens, ducks and white turkeys. The land is now often boggy, and colonised by alder and various willow species, some long-leafed, like the osiers seen on other West Cork islands, possibly introduced for basket-making. The Royal Ferns hereabouts are some of the tallest I've ever seen, rising to seven feet. A marshy field on the left is colonised by horsetails, survivors of a primitive plant family whose ancestors included the giant trees that formed coal deposits millions of years ago. They are poisonous to livestock but the young shoots are considered a delicacy in Japan, and used in medicine for urinary complaints. Grains of silicate in the stems protect them from foraging animals and, in the past, they have been used as sandpaper for shaping wood or bone. They propagate by rhizomes, spreading underground. The stems are jointed, like bamboos, each joint having a whorl of grassy leaves, like tiers of tiny umbrellas.

Grazing is extremely good on Whiddy, and some mainland farmers rent pasture land.

We shortly see the first of the Kilmore Lakes, with reed mace, commonly called bull-rushes, in the wet ground nearby, and water lilies on the surface. The water lily is not an Eastern exotic, but a native plant, its flower the largest in the Irish flora. The stems may be up to nine feet long and were once eaten as a delicacy. Its beauty is fleeting; the flowers open only towards midday but close as evening approaches.

The roadsides now are showpieces of alien invasion, with montbretia from France, knotweed from Japan, and fuchsia from Chile jostling for space.

The second lakes is soon approached; some houses have been sited nearby, to enjoy the fine views. This lake is divided from the sea by a thin strip of land which is regularly inundated. Sea birds are common on the surface, gulls and cormorants, and trout swim beneath. Herons fish in the shallows, and snipe may be flushed from the surrounds. Otters are plentiful. Off the south shore lies a rock with the intriguing name of Lousy Castle Island, but surely even lice would find little sustance in this barren spot. Far beyond are the hills of the Muntervary (Sheep's Head) peninsula.

(6) At the T-junction, we go right. We can, if we have time in hand, go left and stroll down the south side of the lake to the sea, but our itinerary takes us right and goes north west now. The rising ground gives us fine views of the Caha Mountains. A very overgrown path on the left leads down to the remains of a church, possibly pre-12th century, and an ancient graveyard. There is also an early ecclesiastical enclosure and a holy well in this parish.

(7) When we reach another T-junction, we go right again, circling back to the post box and the pier. The road left goes to the deep water oil terminal at Reenaknock. The storage tanks were built in 1960 and hold part of the nation's oil reserves. The Whiddy terminal is inextricably associated with the Betelgeuse disaster.

On 8 January 1979, the French oil tanker Betelgeuse was unloading her cargo of 74,000 tonnes of heavy Arabian crude and 40,000 tonnes of Arabian light oil at the Gulf Oil Terminal when the 40,000 tonnes of light remaining in the vessel's hold exploded, setting it on fire and splitting it into two parts, both of which sank, releasing the 40,000 tonnes of oil into the sea. The jetty and terminal were badly damaged but fortunately the eighteen storage tanks nearby escaped. The 42 crewmen of the Betelgeuse and 7 workers at the terminal died in the explosion. ConocoPhilips maintains a Single Point Mooring at the terminal capable of handling vessels of over 300,000 tons and there is also a jetty where smaller ships discharge.

Nearing the post box and the post-office, it is best to pass the first road on the right (which carries traffic to the terminal) and follow the 'top' road around. We pass the holm oak opposite the Post Office. The trunk is wonderfully gnarled, and is host to luxuriant lichens. These trees are also called live oaks because they are evergreen and 'alive' all year.

Pheasants are common on Whiddy in winter; perhaps they flee the mainland and the shotguns.

The island peace is palpable as we walk down the quay to catch the evening boat; there is not a sound. With the binoculars, we look into the depths alongside the pier and get a close-up view of two-spot gobies, small mid-water swimmers, slowly cruising in the crystal-clear water; they have a conspicuous black spot under the dorsal fin and near the tail, and are a lovely pinkish colour when seen up close. Small pollock also swim about in summer, and sand eels and sprats, followed by schools of mackerel, when the weather is right.

◎ Start point

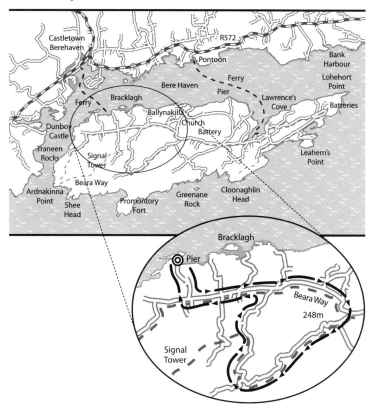

Bere Island Walk

Location, access and island life: Bere Island (OS Sheet 84, centre at squares 7043 and 7143) lies on the north west side of Bantry Bay, off the fishing port of Castletownberehaven. It is reached by ferries from the town quays (15 minutes), and from Pontoon (20 minutes), off the R572 about 4km east of the town. The island is 7 miles (11km) long, by 3 miles (5km) wide, at widest point, and rises to 258m. It has a population of 210 at the time of writing. There is a shop, two pubs, a post office, a restaurant, a B&B and two hostels. There are some good coves for swimming. Ted O'Sullivan's *Bere Island, a Short History* supplied useful material for this walk.

The walk, description and distance: Our route takes us on a round of about 9km, and includes a loop of about 5km off-road. It follows a section of the Beara Way, of which the island can boast some of the loveliest stretches. The scenery is magnificent and a feature is the profusion of wild flowers, possibly because the ditches have never been poisoned with pesticide or flailed by mechanical hedge cutters. The off-road loop is closed on January 31st each year.

Walking conditions: Largely gentle terrain, with one steep sector for about 200m on a rough track. Stout shoes or boots are advisable, especially in damp weather.

An introduction.

Castletownberehaven, where we take the ferry (also called Castletownbere, or simply Castletown) is the 'capital' of the Beara Peninsula, a rugged finger of land extending into the Atlantic. It is the largest fishing port in the south west. Spanish is often heard around the quays, where ranks of big trawlers rock on their moorings, not the Spanish of tourists but of Basque and Gallego fishermen, and truckers from Bilbao and Vigo who come to drive the catch home.

The crossing to Bere Island is made from the town's quays to the island's West Pier, or from Pontoon, 4km west of the town, to Lawrence Cove, near the village of Rerrin, situated at the eastern end. There is a fine loop walk eastward from Rerrin, taking one to a Martello Tower, gun batteries and the peninsula of Leahern's Point. However, as visitors based in Castletown may not have a car, I have described a walk most conveniently reached from the ferry port in the town.

Bere Island is close to shore, but it has the same feeling of apart-ness from the mainland as the further flung islands of West Cork. Looking at it from the sea front of Castletownberehaven, it seems little different in character from the beautiful and rugged coast to east or west but one somehow seems to be walking in another world the moment one steps off the ferry. Why the world across the narrow stretch of water should feel different is a mystery, but whenever we have crossed, the sensation has been the same, a change of air, another country.

As we cross in the ferry, we may contemplate the ruins of Dunboy Castle, on the mainland to the south-west, the shell of a once-fine house of many windows, now stark and empty, the walls and casements ivy-grown. This was the last home of Cam O'Sullivan Beare, the last lord of Beara, who paid the price for his support of the Irish cause at Kinsale in 1601 when the victorious English general, Carew, marched west, burning and levelling all remaining pockets of Irish resistance. So it was with Dunboy. Carew and his regiments approached the castle from Bere Island, and after a siege of eleven days left it in ruins, having slaughtered all within. O'Sullivan fled to Dursey and, after it too was overrun and its people massacred, set off on the bitter march to Leitrim, briefly recounted in the Dursey Island text in this book.

From the deck of the ferry, the narrowness of the western strait between island and mainland can be appreciated. The channel is full of maritime history, much of it lying fathoms deep. To watch the big trawlers heaving and riding on a sea driven by south-westerly gales is to appreciate the force of the funnelled neck of water. Many ships have been wrecked here, although skippered by capable men. When Ireland was a colony, the British fleet sometimes took shelter in the inner road, and gun batteries were maintained on the island until the British presence, begun in 1797, ended in 1938. As we draw close to the pier we pass the Sheep Islands, rocks capped with gorse and heather in late summer, a pretty picture against the mountains of Beara.

Old cottage, now used as a store.

Itinerary.
(1) We begin the walk at the West Pier. Some of the parked cars are falling to pieces where they stand and these, along with a couple of wrecked boats, make the scene picturesque and distinctly not 'mainland'. Nearby, is a modern cafe serving Italian coffee and light meals. There are signs for the Beara Way and Cycle Route.

The road up from the pier is delightfully old-fashioned, the ditches being host to every common wildflower as it comes into season, and to fuchsia, gorse and heather too. All the island ditches are similarly rich in blooms and blossoms; perhaps they have never been subjected to the pesticides or flail saws that mainland road verges suffer annually and as a result, burgeon with flowers and wild shrubs, some seldom seen on the mainland, and a delight to the eye. We pass between well kept houses, with gardens, a shed with a red corrugated roof and a pretty cottage. A ruined Signal Tower is silhouetted on the hill ahead of us, another of the chain of towers built by the English along the south west coast as an early-warning system against a repeat of the attempted French invasion of 1798. Stone walls climb the hill, seemingly dividing fallow land from fallow land to little purpose. Perhaps they were part of a Famine Relief schemes set in place to insure the Irish would earn whatever little help they got.

(2) We arrive at a T-junction and turn left, in the Rerrin direction, also signposted for the Beara Way. We pass a Marian shrine, built in 1954, and from the high ground soon get panoramic views of Castletownbere across the channel. There is a Standing Stone and house ruins in the fields to the right.

The road is tarred, and undulating, with little or no traffic, rising on the right, falling away to the sea on the left. Trees surround the houses, as shelter-belts. We ignore the cross roads, and continue on the straight road east. For a short distance, pines grow on both sides of the road, and then there are fields with gorse and heather, resplendent in late summer. We ignore the turning down to the left and pass fields grazed by sheep before passing the new school, built in 1980, on the left, its perimeter wall painted with scenes from Irish legends by the children. There is a pretty ruin beside it, an old cottage with a rusting, red corrugated roof.

We now see a sign to the left for Ballynakilla and, after crossing Ballynakilla Bridge, we pass the old school - a site with marvellous views - its yard overgrown with rushes, loosestrife, royal fern, montbretia, field scabious, bindweed and a dozen other wildflowers. On the wall to the right of the gate, a sign tells us that in 1828, there were three schools on Bere Islands, the Ballynakilla school being a mud cabin with one teacher and 97 pupils. It was replaced by this building in 1857; in 1928, it still had one hundred pupils, dropping to 39 by 1980, when the new school opened.

Harvesting carageen moss in the rock pools.
It is still used for traditional cures and desserts

Pupil numbers reflect the decline in population on Bere Island. Pre-Famine, in 1841, it was 2,122; ten years later, it was 1,454 and then declined further until works on the island defences and a new market in exporting fish to America offered employment in the first decades of the 20th century. However, it plunged again when the fish market ceased and went into steeper decline after the Second World War. It has stabilised since the millennium and now numbers about 210 residents.

In autumn, the hedges stretching beyond the school are purple with fuchsia, and golden with dwarf gorse and lady's bedstraw - the Bere Island roads could accurately be called Wildflower Walks. Montbretia still blooms in early September, when it is largely gone on the mainland, and the dwarf gorse is in its first flowering, a lovely sight.

We ignore the right turning, climbing the hill. We have spectacular views of the Slieve Miskish Mountains, across the sound; we are opposite Maulin and Knocknagree, with Hungry Hill to the right. The folds are especially

Honeysuckle. Wildflowers are everywhere on Bere.

striking in evening light, when they are defined by deep shadows. An abandoned house, with twin chimneys, stands between us and the channel, sheep grazing in the field of thistles in front, an idyllic scene against the backdrop of sea and mountains.

Now, as we top a rise on the road, there's a pub - roofless, at the time of writing - on the right, and a Martello Tower on a bare hill ahead of us. We ignore the left turning marked Rerrin and the Beara Cycle Route; Greenane is signposted, ahead and there is a roadside map of the island, erected by the Irish Heart Foundation. Pines line the road, with occasionally large trees, sycamore, with red leaf stems and 'helicopter' seed pods, and ash with leaves that move in the breeze like feathers. We ignore another left. The road rises relatively steeply; we can see that it levels off ahead. Unfortunately, there is stand of Japanese knotweed along here on the left; it should be eradicated (if that is possible) before it begins to subsume the marvellous local flora. Amongst a nest of roadside signs, a sign directs us right for the Bere Island Standing Stone and the Lighthouse. We take this. To add three kilometers to the walk, one can continue past the Martello Tower and turn right; the map clearly shows this route.

(3) We walk uphill now, and shortly see the Standing Stone, or gallán, on our left, with a Heritage Plaque telling us that it dates from the Bronze Age 2000 BC to 500 BC, time of the legendary Tuatha de Danann, and that it is said to mark the exact centre of the island. We are now up very high, and get magnificent views of the Standing Stone, the Martello Tower and the huge bulk of Hungry Hill across the water. On the lower slopes, the hill wears a skirt of green; above this, it is brown in dry weather but silvery and magical after rain where the ribs of rock catch the light as they run up to the flat summit. We can see another tower at the eastern end of Bere and, looking across Bantry Bay, the big caves and coves on the southern shore and the tip of the Sheep's Head protruding far into the Atlantic.

Ruin on Bere Island, with the mountains of Beara behind.

(4) Opposite the Standing Stone, we leave the road and take the hill track. A sign tells us this section of the Beara Way is closed on 31st of January each year; no doubt the landowner wishes to assert his rights over the route. A stile gives access. No dogs are allowed; there are sheep loose on the hillside. We can see a cross on the small hill ahead.

Meadowsweet, sweet perfume as we walk the roads in August.

The track curves around; there is nothing but rush and dwarf gorse. The higher we go, the better the views, and it is breathtaking to look down on the world below. At the cross, erected in 1950 to commemorate the Holy Year, we look back and see that there are two small lakes almost between us and the Martello Tower. Shortly afterwards, we reach the top of our gentle climb, and start down. We can no longer see the Sheep's Head; we are looking straight out into the Atlantic where an Air India flight so tragically went down in 1985, blown out of the sky by a terrorist bomb, with a loss of all 329 lives aboard it.

The scenery is wild and rugged, of rock and bog; there is no sign of a house or of a human being. Bird life is scarce too, mainly ravens and rock pipits, but kestrels and peregrine falcons may be seen too. The ruined Signal Tower we saw from the pier is now on a hill ahead of us, and we can see all the way up the coast to Black Ball Head (also with a Signal Tower) and to White Ball Head, with a promontory fort, beyond. The track is good, wide enough for a off-road vehicle. As we start to descend, we have as fine a view of Castletownbere as one could wish for.

(5) The path reaches a T-junction, and we go right. White, daisy-like camomile edges the path in places, still flowering late in the year. We are heading downhill towards the Bere Haven Sound, back to civilisation, the island houses and the town across the water. We pass some pines and reach a surfaced road. Now, to the left, is the continuance of the Beara Way taking

Grey seal pups are left to fend alone at three weeks old. They regularly seek shelter on the coast of Bere Island during storms.

the walker to the west end of the island and then back to the pier; this option can be easily followed on the map and would add about four kilometres to our walk. We ignore the track and continue on the road, passing white gates and a white farmhouse, heading down to Ballynakilla Bridge. The road rises slightly, little used, with grass growing up the middle. A rusting one-time motorhome lies in a field by the road side, wrecked and colourful, sporting the vintage number plate 44 IF.

(6) We reach the dorsal road again at Ballynakilla Bridge, and turn left, walking west to the turning that takes us down to the pier and the ferry to the mainland. It is a short but pleasant voyage, especially of a summer evening with the sun setting behind Slieve Miskish and mackerel breaking the water around the boat.

◎ Start point

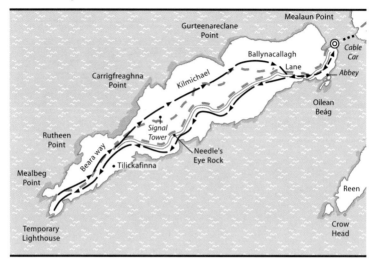

Dursey Island Walk

Location, access and island life: Dursey Island lies at the extreme western end of the Beara Peninsula, 24km beyond Castletownbere. Above Ballaghboy Pier (OS Sheet 84, 508418), a cable car crosses the Sound to the island, which is 6.4 km (4 miles) long, and a maximum of 2.4km (1.5 miles) wide. It rises to 825 feet at the highest point of the dorsal ridge that runs from east to west. On the south side of the ridge, there are three small settlements; the island's field are clustered around or between these. At the time of writing, locals tell me there are about eight permanent residents, with a handful more coming and going to tend to the farm animals, or for summer holidays to one of the few renovated cottages. The north side of the ridge slopes more steeply to the sea, a landscape of bracken, gorse and heather which is grazed by sheep and goats but offers little shelter or pasture. There is no shop, overnight accommodation or public phone on Dursey. There is a post box; mail is collected and taken to the cable car.

I am privileged to have Penny Durell's *Discover Dursey* to hand, a small volume replete with information. Therein are recorded the myths, legends and place names of Dursey, the pre-history and history, the stories of pirates and privateers, the local belief that Bonnie Prince Charlie was sheltered there while returning to Scotland from long exile in France, tales of brave sea rescues, of the destruction of the first lighthouse in massive storms, of fishing the kind sea and farming the harsh land, of evictions and endurance, shipwrecks and maritime mishaps. Also included is a comprehensive list of the flora and fauna, the text of old poems and songs and a guide to the island's antiquities. With detailed maps and fine colour plates *Discover Dursey* is worth reading even if one never took the cable car.

The walk, description and distance: The walk on Dursey is about 20km, or 12 miles, but one doesn't feel the distance and there are many shorter, but nonetheless interesting, options. Our route follows the Beara Way, taking the island's only road from the cable car terminal at the eastern end to the far western end, where for the last mile it becomes a track. We return to the cable car via a path that runs parallel to the road but taking higher ground. The air is heady with ozone, the views are marvellous, the flora and fauna is specialised and interesting, and there are various historical sites, some of great antiquity.

Walking conditions: The outward leg is on tarred road or grass. The return route, through gorse and heather, up hill and down dale, is never so arduous as to be beyond the capacity of the average Sunday walker. Stout shoes or boots are recommended, as the off road sections are rough in places.

An introduction.

Dursey is different than the relatively sheltered islands of Roaring Water and Bantry Bay. There are no hedgerow-skirted lanes and no wild trees, although some cottages have small shelter belts of shrubs, sycamore and low pines. t is a high island, and surely one of the loveliest of the West Cork isles. It affords marvellous walking, with no hindrance to the rambler on the traffic-less roads and unfenced hills. The views are always memorable, with bird's eye prospects of the island below us, of the blue mountains of Kerry across the expanse of the Kenmare River - actually an enormous bay -or south, across Bantry Bay, to the finger of hills that is the Sheep's Head peninsula.

Dursey is spectacular in a bare, ascetic way. In winter, the landscape is brown and sere, and the sea grey beneath its steep cliffs and coves. It is romantic when curtains of soft rain blow across the small green fields and ruined cottages. It is sunbaked in good summers, for there are no trees, and no shade. It is loveliest of all in September, when our native gorse is in flower and its rolling hills are dressed in brilliant gold, dramatic against the deep blue of the sea.

But for all its beauty, Dursey has a tragic history. In 1602, after the Irish defeat at Kinsale, its three hundred inhabitants, all members of the O'Sullivan clan, were massacred, and all of Beara was put to fire and sword. Finally, in the freezing winter of that year, the chieftain, Donal Cam O'Sullivan Beare, led what was left of his people on a long ghost-march to refuge with their O'Rourke kinsmen in far off Leitrim, harried and attacked by both English and Irish every mile of the way. Of the one thousand men women and children that set out, only thirty

A Dursey ruin. Once, the island was densely inhabited.

five reached their destination. In 2003, their journey was recreated in "The March", a film by David Bickley for RTE. More of this history can be found in the Bere Island walk in this book.

We reach Dursey by Ireland's only cable car, crossing the abyss between the headland and the island in a stout but small box suspended eighty feet above the boiling sea. In the narrow cliff-walled channel of the Sound, two currents meet. When one reflects that Dursey is, in fact, the severed fingertip of the Beara Peninsula, it is not surprising that the waters of vast Kenmare Bay and even vaster Bantry Bay, spilling through the gap between the island and the land, should clash and boil. The sea is, most often, crystal clear. Dolphins disport within and outside the Sound, and are worth watching for.

The crossing is a novel and exciting trip. Immediately after setting off, the car, which takes six passengers, starts 'downhill', that is, towards the rocks far below. Seconds later, to general relief, it straightens to the horizontal and pursues a stately, level course to the other side. It is a crossing well-worthwhile for its own sake; and the delights of the island await on the other side.

Itinerary.

(1) We set off from the Cable Car landing place; the car was installed in 1969, inspired by a local man who had rigged up a pulley to transfer his sheep across the abyss. The landing place is known as Aít an Fheoir, the site of the massacre. Here, in June 1602, Carew's soldiers paraded children pinioned on their spears, shot and hacked islanders to death and roped others together in groups and pushed them over the cliffs into the sea.

The open road ahead rises gently. In September, with the gorse on bloom, it crosses a landscape of gold. A path runs down to the left, to the pier. Until the cable car, this was the point of access but in winter months it was often cut off for days or weeks at a time.

Now, below us on the left we clearly see the monastery and burial ground, once known as St Mary's Abbey, perched above the sea. Philip O'Sullivan Beare, born on Dursey, wrote of the island during his long exile in Spain where he was a foremost scholar and a commander of the navy. He relates that the monastery was founded by one Bonaventure, a Spanish bishop who held the See of Ross, but it is likely that a much earlier chapel existed on the site. Amongst the graves is the tomb of the descendants of the O'Sullivan chieftains of Beara, the first interred in 1787, and the last of the family to live on Dursey, who was buried in 1977. There are also a number of older, unmarked graves. The building was already in ruins in 1602, when Carew's soldiers used it for cover while attacking the Oileán Beag, close by.

The Oileán Beag is dramatically separated from Dursey by a steep-sided channel, once spanned by a drawbridge. A castle and fortifications were installed by Philip O'Sullivan's father, Diarmuid, in the late sixteenth century. Carew's forces levelled these in 1602, and the defenders and civilians who had taken refuge there were slaughtered.

The monastery and burial ground, once known as St Mary's Abbey.

The road is unfenced, with grass growing down the middle. We pass a parking space where islanders leave their cars when they take the cable car to Ireland. Dursey casts a spell from the moment one arrives. We are in a dimension removed from the everyday world, as if we are back in the nineteen forties, with little changed except the metaling of the roads and the electricity power lines, recently installed. A few more slates are gone off the roofs of the ruins, many of them abandoned even then.

Topping the rise, we see the Signal Tower on the island's highest hill: it is a constant presence, silhouetted against the sky. The road climbs steeply to the hamlet of Ballynacallagh, a dozen or so houses, some renovated, some in ruins, and small outhouses with tin roofs painted red. The house clusters on Dursey are all attractive. The houses are almost all the same, single storey but tall, with steeply pitched, slate roofs and chimneys at either end. Happily, restorations have not changed their character. They are, largely, grey, of stone, melding into the landscape; some are whitewashed, in the old tradition. They enjoy magnificent views.

Dursey, gorse and heather;in September, its rolling hills are dressed in gold.

(2) Beyond the hamlet, we pass the island post box, somewhat rusted, and walk downhill, passing small fields divided by stone walls. Ahead, we see the settlement of Kilmichael. Ruins on the hillside above us include the school. Lewis's *Topographical Dictionary* of Cork puts the population of Dursey at 198 in 1837, before the Famine, and it was still 131 in 1943. However, due to emigration, the Dursey school closed for want of pupils in 1975. At Kilmichael, free-range chickens scratch along the roadside.

A kilometre beyond the village, a turf-cutters' road goes up to the right. We will meet this in the high lands later. We round a bend and soon pass through a gate. The road now narrows, with a cliff face on one side and a hair-raising drop into the sea on the other. Rocks, fallen from above, lie against the cliff on our right. One rock, called the Needle's Eye, is split forming a narrow passage. Legend had it that if a newly-wed girl passed through the fissure three times from east to west, she would not die in childbirth.

Soon, we can see, far off, the stump of the lighthouse on the Calf Rock, at the western end. We pass fields enclosed by stone walls (the stones were cleared from the fields, so the walls were dual-purpose) running, in parallel, down to the shore. Tilickafinna hamlet has a scatter of some six houses, all facing south, a few renovated. The house of ornithologist Dr Derek Scott and his wife demonstrates that some shrubs can succeed despite the prevailing, salt-laden south westerlies.

(3) We pass through a gap in a stone wall and, leaving the last house on the island behind, we go through a gate onto a green road curving gracefully

The Signal Tower on Cnoc Mór, an early-warning system against French invasion, 1804.

uphill and taking us to a scalp from which we look down on the green sward of the western headland, grazed by sheep. The views are magnificent, Iveragh, with the Ring Of Kerry, to the north, blue mountains behind blue mountains and, offshore, Scariff and Deenish islands, the one green and hump-backed like the Great Blasket, the other bare and angular like Small Skellig. Near in, to the north, are The Cow, and then the Bull Rock, with its gleaming lighthouse. Through binoculars, both seem almost clouded in birds; indeed, they are amongst the ten most important coastal bird sites in Ireland, the Bull Rock being Ireland's second largest gannetry, with over 1,500 breeding pairs, while both islands host breeding storm petrels, guillemot, razorbill, fulmar and other species. Here on the headlands, we may also enjoy the sight of choughs soaring and tumbling overhead, with black glossy feathers and red beaks and legs, and peregrine falcons may be seen here too.

Footworn paths now take us over the headland's crown and down a steep slope to the Temporary Lighthouse which, after the sea destroyed the Calf Rock light in 1881, warned off shipping until the Bull Rock lighthouse was completed. The Calf, The Cow and The Bull have long been a danger to seafarers. Waves have been seen to entirely engulf The Cow, standing 64m (205ft) above the sea. Such waves took away the top of the cast iron tower on the Calf Rock light in November 1881, forcing the three keepers, and three workmen, to flee to a concrete bunker where, for twelve days, they were trapped in a tiny space, the sea raging over them. Numerous attempts to reach them were defeated by the strength of the storms. In an earlier tempest, in 1869, seven local men had bravely rowed out under the mistaken impression that the keepers had signalled for rescue, and all had been drowned. The Bull Rock light came into service in 1889. The rock is riven by a tunnel cave, large enough for a trawler to pass through, but it should have been obvious that, at almost 100m (330ft) above the sea, it was a much more favourable site than The Calf, at only 24m (78ft) above water.

Weather permitting, this western end of Dursey is a fine spot to perch for an hour and contemplate the western ocean. Maritime history is close by, above the waves and beneath them. Even on halcyon days, there is often a small breeze while, out of the wind, it can be as warm as the Mediterranean. No cars, no sound; white waves breaking in silent animation on black rocks under the Bull light. Far below us, squadrons of gannets fly over the stiff, blue sea, their white plumage catching the sunlight. In late summer, when the mackerel are inshore, they rocket like missiles onto the shoals, raising white water.

(4) With splendid views of sea, islands and distant mountains, we turn and begin the return leg of our walk. Our landmark, now, is the Signal Tower silhouetted on top of Cnoc Mór (The Big Hill), to the east. The Beara Way markers guide one to a path meandering up to the summit at 252m (819ft). Penny Durrel reports that islanders would light bonfires here to bid farewell to sons or daughters passing on emigrant ships to America. The tower was started in 1804, and possibly never completed. It was part of a chain of towers, each visible from the one before and after, built along the coast in response to English fears of a more determined French incursion than that of 1796 into Bantry Bay. The work was still in desultory progress in 1811 but, finally habitable, it was manned for only a few years, the threat of the French having abated. Standing thirty feet tall, it has survived similar towers elsewhere and, for some years, was a social centre for the islanders. The views are outstanding. Bantry Bay opens to the south, with Sheep's Head and the Mizen Head, beyond. Northwards, in clear weather we may see the Skellig Rocks, redoubt of the early Irish church, off the coast of Kerry; even the distant Blaskets may be seen on a fine day. The island itself is laid out below us.

(5) Beyond the tower, our route starts downhill. There is evidence of turf-cutting. We cross a wide track, running from the south shore to the north, where there is a *fulacht fiadh* site, a Bronze Age cooking place. Following the Beara Way (at Way Mark No 66, a stile) we reach a lag between the hills and some flat, boggy ground. From here, we can see the white swathe of Ballydonegan Strand, and Allihies, on the mainland. The way-marked path climbs again, skirting the next low hill on its northern side.

On the descent, we encounter a steep slope for 50m or so, the houses of Kilmichael below us on the right. We arrive at a track running along a stone wall; it goes right to Kilmichael but we go left, crossing a bridge over a narrow stream. We meet a stone wall beautifully colonised by white lichens, with sheep wire on top (WM No. 72). A stile bridges this. The route takes us around a corner of the wall and we are on a green path, part of the old bog road to the turf cuttings (WM No. 75). The high ground is now on our left; between us and the sea, fields, with cattle. Butterflies, especially Small Heaths, Meadow Browns and Ringlets are abundant here, but they are everywhere on the island. Pied wagtails are also a feature and swallows in summer, using Kilmichael's ruins for nesting places.

The main road of Dursey, with the Signal Tower against the sky.

(6) The path swings sharply right, descending to a gate. Passing through it, we are walking down a lane, into Ballynacallagh village. On the stone walls, bell heather and ling thrive (the ling is pink, the heather, purple) along with wall rue, stone crop, foxgloves and fuchsia; there is Japanese knotweed in a garden, perhaps once sown as a decorative plant but now, as usual, subsuming all other growth. At the T-junction, we meet the road, and go left for the cable car.

As we await its arrival, we notice the Beara Way Marks marching northward over the headland across the Sound.

FERRIES AND CABLE CAR TO THE ISLANDS

These schedules are not written in stone, and the author cannot guarantee them. From year to year, and depending on weather, they may change. The ferries to the bigger islands are a regular service but to the smaller islands, and to Dursey, the crossings, to some extent, depend on the demand. This is understandable. The operators provide a safe and reliable service but if there's nobody waiting on the opposite pier, there's no point in wasting the diesel. So, if travelling out of season, it is well, where possible, to ring the ferryman, just to be sure to be sure.

HEIR

• From Cunnamore Pier, 5 minutes.

Cunnamore Pier is reached by turning south at Church Cross,
between Skibbereen and Ballydehob, on the N71.
Ferry times are posted at the pier.

For info. phone Richard Pyburn or John Moore 086 8092447 see also
www.heirisland.com

• From Baltimore and Schull

Heir is also served by the occasional
but irregular inter-island ferries. The ITB office at Skibbereen,
phone. 028 21766, open all year, may be able to advise.

SHERKIN

• From Baltimore, approx. 15 mins.

Between June 1st and October 1st, up to 10 ferries each day,
the earliest on weekdays leave at 07:45 and the latest return at 20:45.
Less frequent crossings in winter.

For information, phone 028 20218/087 2447828/087 9117377
or Bushe's Bar, 028 20125

CAPE

• From Baltimore, approx. 45 mins.

All year: winter approx. 3 sailings a day; summer, up to 5 sailings a day.
Tel. 028 39159/086 2662197 or consult www.capeclearferry.info

• From Schull, approx. 45 mins. May, June, July, August, Sept. only
Tel. 028 28278 or 087 2379302 for info.

LONG

• From Colla Pier, 10 minutes.

Colla is 3km south of Schull on the road following the coast.

Summer schedule (from July 1st) 11:30 - 14:30 - 16:30 .
Otherwise, phone John Shelley, Tel 028 28470.

WHIDDY

• From Bantry town, approx. 15 mins.

Mon. Wed. Fri. Dep. Bantry 09:30 - 11:30 - 14:40 - 16:00 - 18:00
Dep. Whiddy 08:30 - 11:00 - 14:00 - 15:35 - 17:45
Tues. Thurs. Dep. Bantry 09:30 - 14:40 - 16:00 - 18:00
[+ 1100 June July Aug]
Dep. Whiddy 08:30 - 14:00 - 15:35 - 17:45
Saturday Dep. Bantry 09:30 - 11:00 - 14:00 - 18:00
Dep. Whiddy 09:00 - 10:45 - 13:45 - 18:45
Sunday & Bank Holidays Dep. Bantry 11:00 - 14:00 - 18:00
Dep. Whiddy 11:15 - 14:15 - 15:35 - 17:45
Tel. Tim O'Leary 027 50310/086 8626734

olearywhiddy@eircom.net

BERE

• From Castletownbere 15 minutes

June 1st to Sept 21st
8 crossings a day, 5 on Sundays,
earliest leaves at 08:00hrs weekdays, latest returns at 20:00hrs.

Sept 22nd to May 31st
7 crossings a day, 3 on Sundays.
Earliest and latest crossings as above.

Tel. Bere Island Ferries 027 75009/ 086 2423140
www.bereislandferries.com

• From Pontoon (20 minutes), off the R572, 4km east of the town.

Sept to May: 8 crossings a day, 6 on Sundays,
earliest leaves at 08:00hrs weekdays, latest returns at 20:00hrs.

Tel. Murphy's Ferry Service 027 75014/087 2386095

www.murphysferry.com

DURSEY

• Cable car from above Ballaghboy Pier. 5 minutes.
All Year. Capacity max. 6 persons.

Monday to Saturday - Depart 09:00 - 14:30 - 19:00

Return - 10:30 - 16:30 - 19:30

Sunday - Depart - 09:00 - 13:00 - 16:00 - 19:00

Return - 10:00, 14:00 (June, July, August) 16:30 - 19:30

Please attend 30 mins before closing time

Notes